OFFICIAL SQA PAST PAPERS WITH ANSWERS

ADVANCED HIGHER

BIOLOGY 2006-2009

BrightRED PUBLISHING

First exam published in 2006.
Published by Bright Red Publishing Ltd, 6 Stafford Street, Edinburgh EH3 7AU
tel: 0131 220 5804 fax: 0131 220 6710 info@brightredpublishing.co.uk www.brightredpublishing.co.uk

ISBN 978-1-84948-072-7

A CIP Catalogue record for this book is available from the British Library.

Bright Red Publishing is grateful to the copyright holders, as credited on the final page of the book, for permission to use their material. Every effort has been made to trace the copyright holders and to obtain their permission for the use of copyright material. Bright Red Publishing will be happy to receive information allowing us to rectify any error or omission in future editions.

ADVANCED HIGHER

2006

[BLANK PAGE]

X007/701

NATIONAL QUALIFICATIONS 2006

TUESDAY, 23 MAY
1.00 PM – 3.30 PM

BIOLOGY ADVANCED HIGHER

SECTION A—Questions 1–25 (25 marks)

Instructions for completion of Section A are given on *Page two*.

SECTIONS B AND C

The answer to each question should be written in ink in the answer book provided. Any additional paper (if used) should be placed inside the front cover of the answer book.

Rough work should be scored through.

Section B (55 marks)

All questions should be attempted. Candidates should note that Question 7 contains a choice.

Question 1 is on Pages 10, 11 and 12. Questions 2, 3 and 4 are on Page 13. Pages 12 and 13 are fold-out pages.

Section C (20 marks)

Candidates should attempt the questions in one unit **either** Biotechnology **or** Animal Behaviour **or** Physiology, Health and Exercise.

LI X007/701 6/4970

Read carefully

1 Check that the answer sheet provided is for **Biology Advanced Higher (Section A)**.

2 For this section of the examination you must use an **HB pencil** and, where necessary, an eraser.

3 Check that the answer sheet you have been given has **your name**, **date of birth**, **SCN** (Scottish Candidate Number) and **Centre Name** printed on it.

Do not change any of these details.

4 If any of this information is wrong, tell the Invigilator immediately.

5 If this information is correct, **print** your name and seat number in the boxes provided.

6 The answer to each question is **either** A, B, C or D. Decide what your answer is, then, using your pencil, put a horizontal line in the space provided (see sample question below).

7 There is **only one correct** answer to each question.

8 Any rough working should be done on the question paper or the rough working sheet, **not** on your answer sheet.

9 At the end of the exam, put the **answer sheet for Section A inside the front cover of this answer book**.

Sample Question

Which of the following molecules contains six carbon atoms?

A Glucose

B Pyruvic acid

C Ribulose biphosphate

D Acetyl coenzyme A

The correct answer is **A**—Glucose. The answer **A** has been clearly marked in **pencil** with a horizontal line (see below).

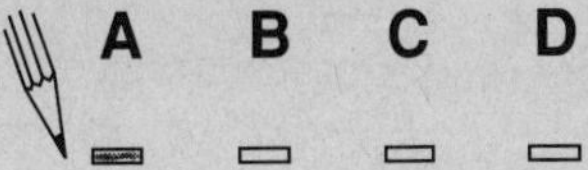

Changing an answer

If you decide to change your answer, carefully erase your first answer and using your pencil, fill in the answer you want. The answer below has been changed to **D**.

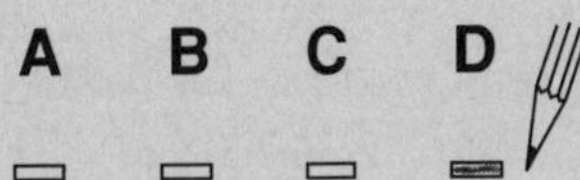

SECTION A

All questions in this section should be attempted.

Answers should be given on the separate answer sheet provided.

1. The presence of which of the following would indicate that a cell was from a plant?

A Plasmodesmata

B Ribosomes

C Cell wall

D Nucleoid

2. Cytokinins are used in plant tissue culture to

A promote totipotency

B promote differentiation

C produce pathogen-free plants

D fuse protoplasts.

3. In solution, glucose molecules exist in three forms. The chemical equilibrium between the forms is shown below.

linear form 0·02% ⟷ α-glucose 38% ⟷ β-glucose 62%

Approximately how many molecules will be in the β-glucose form for every one molecule in the linear form?

A 30

B 300

C 3000

D 30 000

4. The diagram below shows the first two nucleotides in a DNA strand.

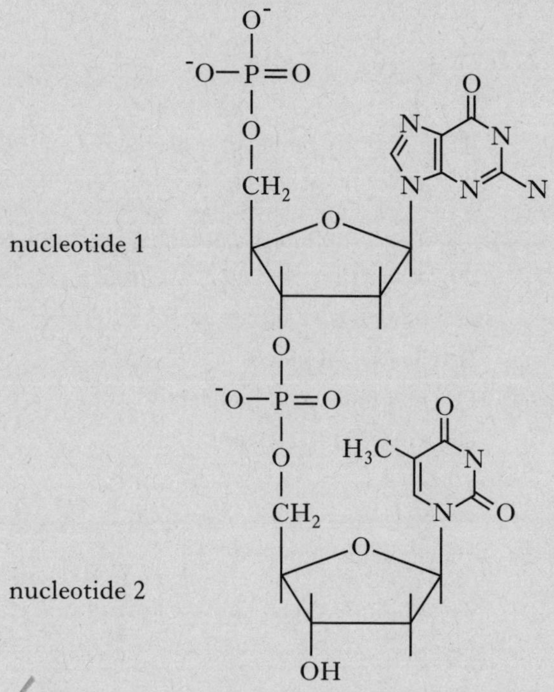

nucleotide 1

nucleotide 2

Which of the following statements about the DNA strand is correct?

Nucleotide 1 is at the

A 3′ end and has the base guanine

B 3′ end and has the base thymine

C 5′ end and has the base guanine

D 5′ end and has the base thymine.

5. At the end of each human chromosome there is a region of DNA known as the telomere that initially consists of 2000 repeats of the sequence TTAGGG. At each mitosis, 100 base pairs are lost from the telomere.

What is the minimum number of mitotic divisions that will completely remove the telomeres?

A 60

B 120

C 240

D 330

[Turn over

6. The percentage of adenine bases in a double strand of DNA is known. For how many of the other bases could the percentage be calculated?

A None

B One

C Two

D Three

7. During DNA replication one of the strands of DNA (the lagging strand) is replicated as a series of fragments that are then bonded together. The enzymes that make and bond the DNA fragments are

A polymerase and ligase

B ligase and kinase

C polymerase and nuclease

D kinase and nuclease.

8. The diagram below shows the arrangement of four proteins (R, S, T and V) and the phospholipid bilayer of a cell membrane.

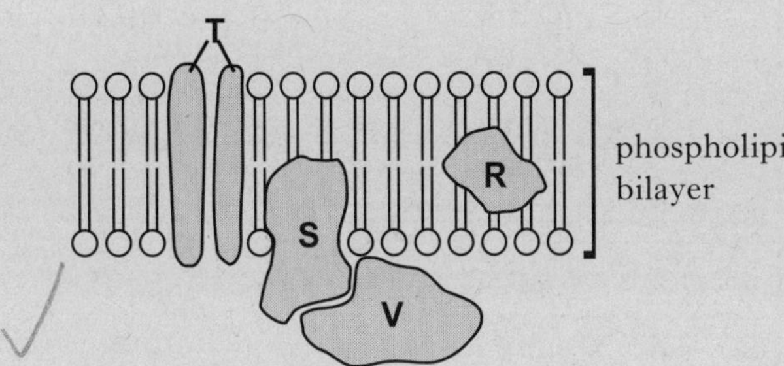

Which of the proteins shown are integral membrane proteins?

A R only

B R and S only

C R, S and T only

D R, S, T and V

9. The mechanism of action of the sodium-potassium pump involves the following stages:

P membrane protein is phosphorylated

Q sodium ions bind to membrane protein

R sodium ions are released

S membrane protein changes conformation

The correct sequence is

A P, Q, R, S

B P, Q, S, R

C Q, P, R, S

D Q, P, S, R.

10. The graph below shows the mass of product resulting from an enzyme-controlled reaction.

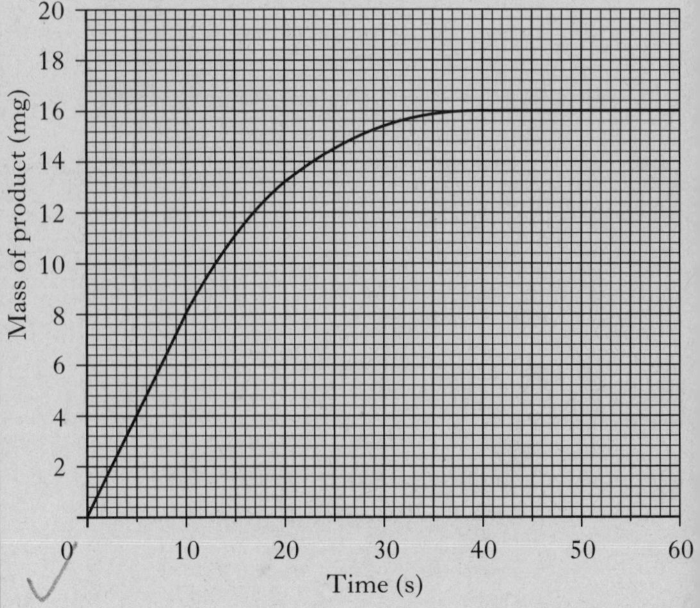

What is the initial rate of reaction?

A $0{\cdot}35\ mg\,s^{-1}$

B $0{\cdot}8\ mg\,s^{-1}$

C $1{\cdot}25\ mg\,s^{-1}$

D $3{\cdot}5\ mg\,s^{-1}$

11. The diagram below illustrates the action of a signalling molecule.

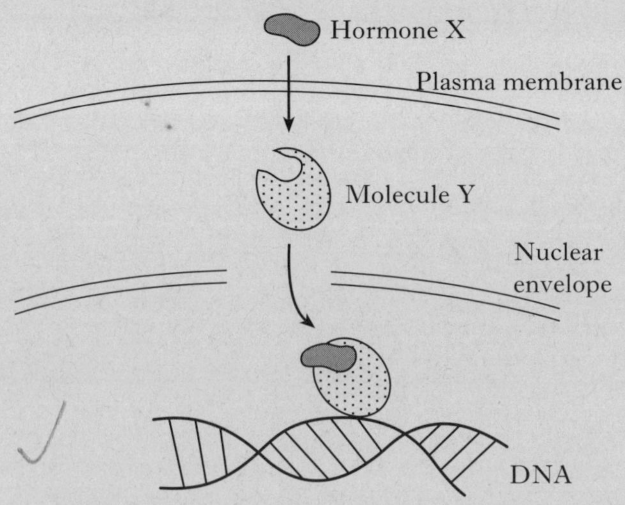

Which line in the table correctly identifies molecules X and Y?

	Hormone X	*Molecule Y*
A	testosterone	regulatory protein
B	insulin	receptor protein
C	insulin	regulatory protein
D	testosterone	receptor protein

12. A forensic scientist is reconstructing the DNA profile of a missing person from analysis of DNA profiles of close relatives. In this case a father of four children is missing. All the children have the same biological mother and father. Results from a single locus probe DNA profile analysis for the four children and their mother are shown below.

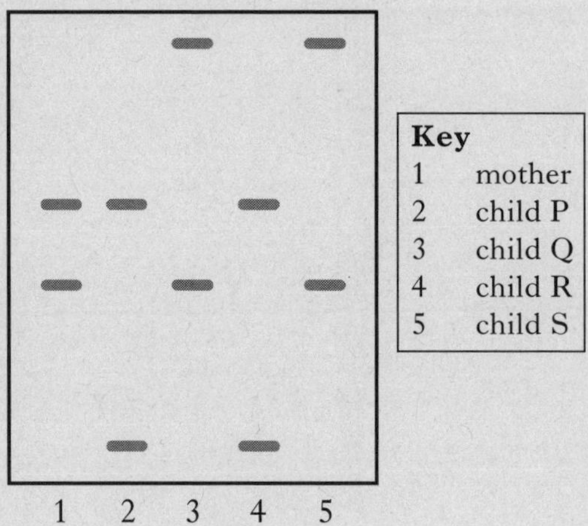

Which of the following is likely to be the DNA profile of the missing father?

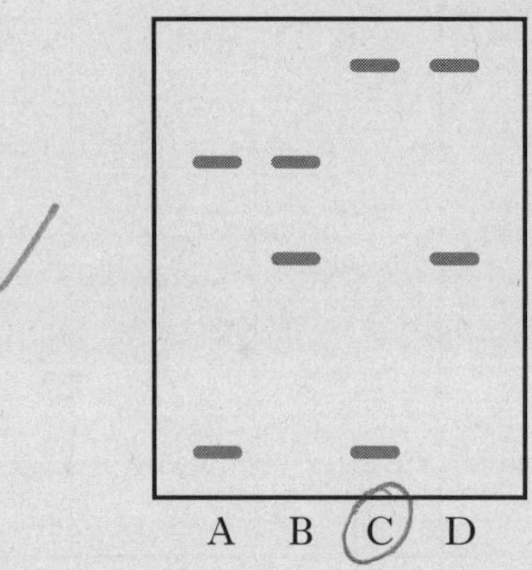

13. The table below shows mean values for net primary productivity (NPP) for four ecosystems.

Ecosystem	*NPP* (kJ m^{-2} yr^{-1})
Desert scrub	1400
Tropical rainforest	36 000
Temperate deciduous forest	22 000
Temperate monoculture	30 000

Which of the following factors is **not** likely to account for these differences?

A Mean annual temperature

B Annual rainfall

C Application of fertiliser

D Carbon dioxide content of air

14. Young bluegill sunfish feed on *Daphnia* (water fleas).

The following table shows how low and high prey densities affect the diet of these fish.

	Low prey density			*High prey density*		
Prey size	*small*	*medium*	*large*	*small*	*medium*	*large*
Percentage available	33	33	34	14	30	56
Percentage eaten	32	33	35	3	40	57

From the information above, which of the following describes the feeding strategy of young bluegill sunfish at different prey density?

	Low prey density	*High prey density*
A	non-selective	non-selective
B	non-selective	selective
C	selective	non-selective
D	selective	selective

15. Which line in the table may be correctly applied to detritivores?

	Mode of nutrition	*Effect on humus production*
A	saprotrophic	increased
B	saprotrophic	decreased
C	heterotrophic	increased
D	heterotrophic	decreased

16. In the nitrogen cycle, which process converts ammonium ions into a form that can be assimilated by producers?

A Nitrification

B Denitrification

C Ammonification

D Nitrogen fixation

[Turn over

17. Several grassland plots were fenced to exclude voles, which feed mainly on annual grasses. The table below shows information about plants in fenced and unfenced plots after two years.

	Relative biomass (units)		*Number of plant species*	
	Fenced plots	*Unfenced plots*	*Fenced plots*	*Unfenced plots*
Annual grasses	120	40	6	6
Other plants	40	80	12	24

Which line of the table below best summarises the effects of excluding voles?

	Productivity of plant community	*Diversity of plant community*
A	increased	increased
B	decreased	increased
C	increased	decreased
D	decreased	decreased

18. The graph below shows the relationship between water temperature and muscle temperature for three species of tuna. Tuna are poikilothermic fish but have some ability to thermoregulate.

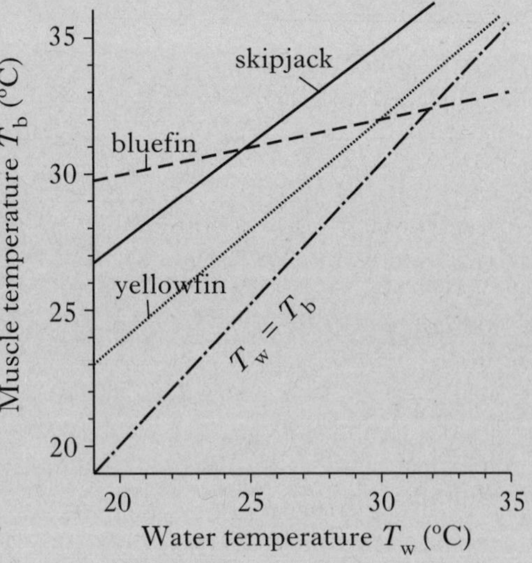

At which environmental temperature would the best thermoregulator have the same muscle temperature as a perfect thermoconformer?

A 24 °C

B 29 °C

C 30 °C

D 32 °C

19. Diagram A shows three burrowing animals which live at different depths on Scottish beaches. They are eaten by various wading birds such as those illustrated in Diagram B.

Diagram A

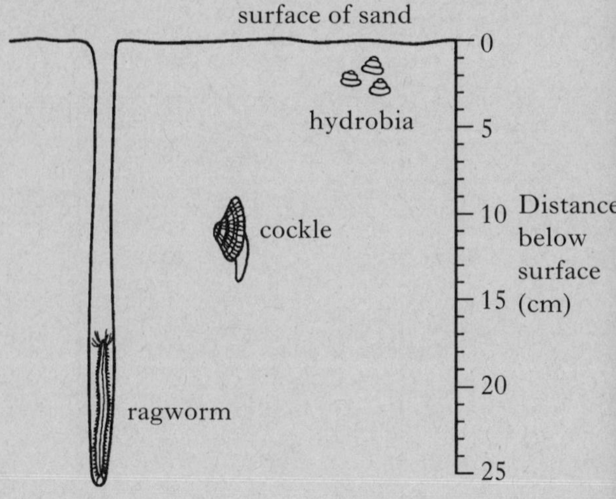

Diagram B

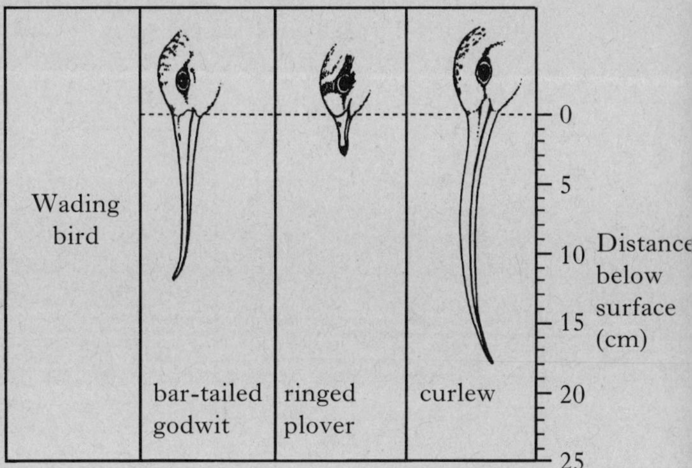

Which of the following is a consequence of the different length of the waders' beaks?

A Competitive exclusion

B Resource partitioning

C Exploitation competition

D Fundamental niche modification

20. The information below shows how several factors are affected by the presence of a hedge. Comparisons can be made with hedges of any height (H). At different distances from the hedge, the value of each factor is calculated as a percentage of its value in an open field. *Relative distance from hedge* is the distance in metres as a multiple of the hedge height H.

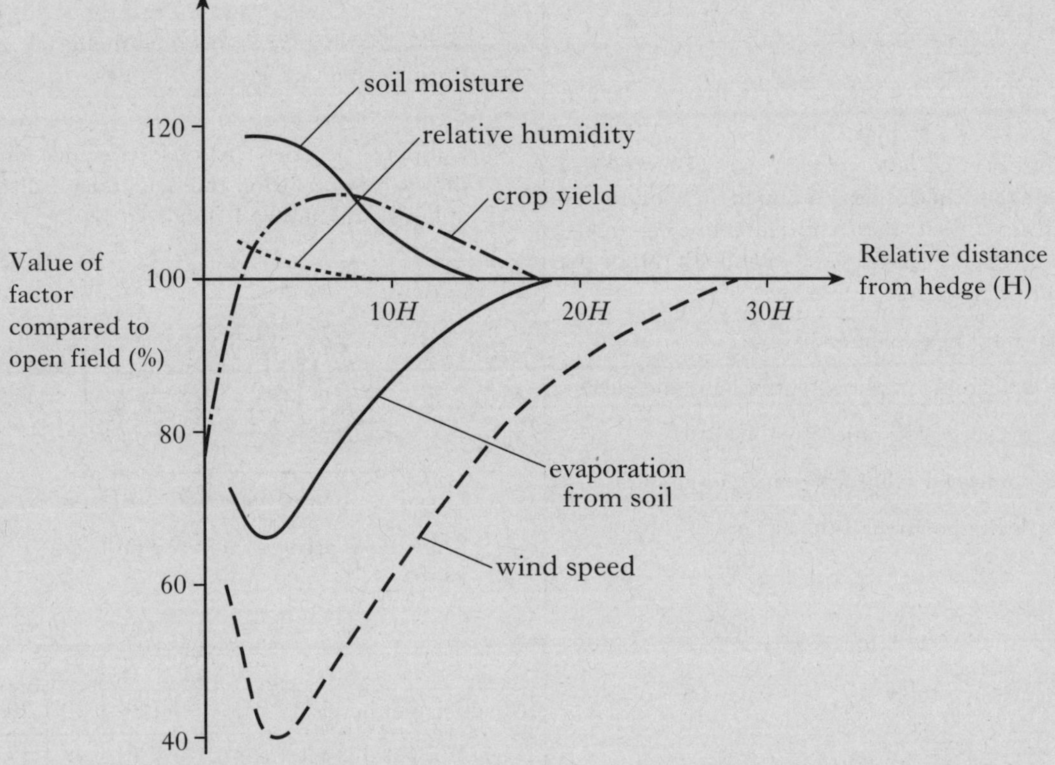

Which of the following is **not** likely to be responsible for an increase in crop yield 30 metres away from a 3 metre high hedge?

A Decreased evaporation from the soil

B Increased soil moisture

C Decreased wind speed

D Increased relative humidity

21. Which line in the table correctly describes ecological niches?

	Fundamental niche	*Realised niche*	*Reason for difference*
A	Resources a species actually uses	Resources a species potentially can use	Interspecific competition
B	Resources a species actually uses	Resources a species potentially can use	Intraspecific competition
C	Resources a species potentially can use	Resources a species actually uses	Interspecific competition
D	Resources a species potentially can use	Resources a species actually uses	Intraspecific competition

22. The giant bullfrog of southern Africa lives in an environment where hot and dry conditions can occur at any time of the year. To survive these conditions the frogs become dormant.

Which combination of terms applies to this type of dormancy?

A Predictive and aestivation

B Predictive and hibernation

C Consequential and aestivation

D Consequential and hibernation

[Turn over

23. Which of the following gases is **both** a greenhouse gas and acidic?

A Carbon dioxide

B Ozone

C CFC

D Methane

24. A large accumulation of algae was observed in a canal that had been polluted by inorganic fertilisers washed in from surrounding fields. The biochemical oxygen demand (BOD) of the water then began to increase.

This could be explained by

A a decrease in photosynthesis by the algae

B reduced respiration by the algae

C decreased solubility of oxygen

D decomposition of the algae.

25. Limpets are invertebrates which attach themselves firmly to rocks on seashores when the tide goes out. Limpet shape seems to be influenced by the degree of exposure to waves the animals experience in their specific locations. On exposed shores, the shells have a "flatter" shape than on sheltered shores because they are less likely to be dislodged by wave action.

Limpet "flatness" was determined on four shores by measuring the heights and diameters of limpets as shown below.

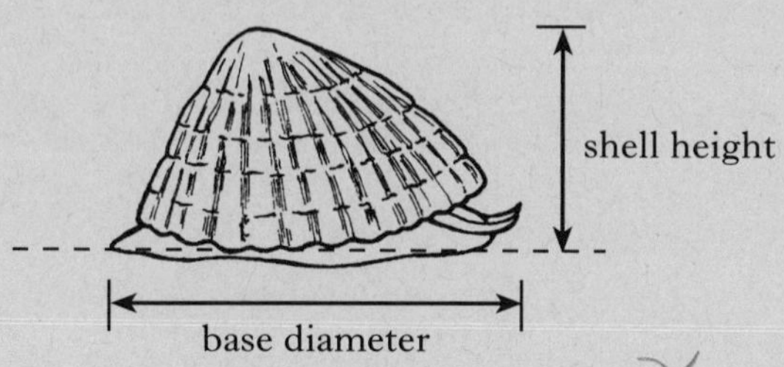

The results are shown in the table.

	Shore			
	A	*B*	*C*	*D*
Mean limpet height (mm)	24	23	20	25
Mean limpet diameter (mm)	40	49	37	50

Which shore is likely to be the most exposed?

[*END OF SECTION A*]

Candidates are reminded that the answer sheet MUST be returned INSIDE the front cover of the answer book.

[Turn over for Section B on *Page ten*

SECTION B

All questions in this section should be attempted.
All answers must be written clearly and legibly in ink.

1. Bovine spongiform encephalopathy (BSE) and variant Creutzfeldt-Jakob disease (vCJD) are examples of fatal brain disease that can pass from one species to another. The nature of the infectious agent is as yet unidentified but, in both diseases, a protein known as PrP^{SC} accumulates in brain tissue.

It has been shown that PrP^{SC} is an altered form of the normal membrane protein PrP^{C}. Both molecules have the same primary structure (PrP) but they differ in how the PrP protein folds. Molecules of PrP^{SC} have a lower proportion of α-helix and a higher proportion of β-sheets. Proteins are normally broken down after a certain length of time by intracellular enzymes. However, the increased β-sheet content makes PrP^{SC} more resistant to enzymatic breakdown, which leads to its accumulation.

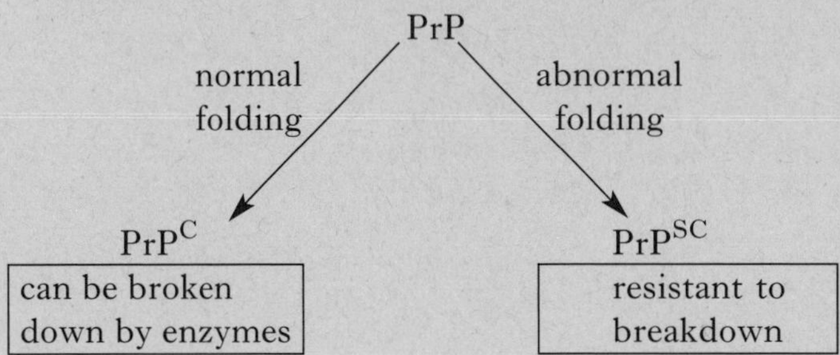

A substance capable of breaking β-sheets (β-breaker) was tested to find out if it could make PrP^{SC} more susceptible to the intracellular enzymes. PrP^{SC} samples from mice and humans were each incubated for 48 hours with different concentrations of β-breaker and the percentage of PrP^{SC} remaining after digestion was determined. The results are shown in the Figure. The error bars in the Figure indicate the degree of variation between replicates.

In the same study, mouse PrP^{SC} was further analysed to determine if any change in the proportions of α-helix and β-sheet had occurred. The results are shown in Table 1.

In a second study, mice were treated with infectious material containing (i) PrP^{SC} and (ii) a 1 : 1 mixture of PrP^{SC} and β-breaker. Quantities of PrP^{SC} were equivalent in both treatments. Table 2 shows the mean time to onset of symptoms of brain disease in the two groups. Different concentrations of PrP^{SC} were prepared by diluting stock solutions.

Question 1 (continued)

Figure: The effect of β-breaker on mouse and human PrP^{SC}.

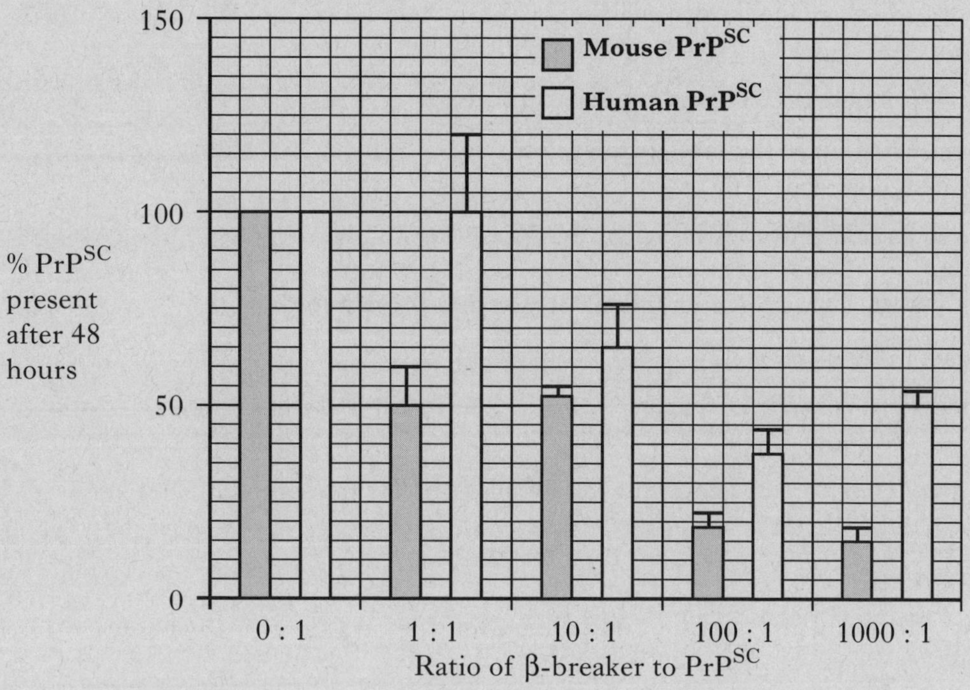

Table 1: Proportions of secondary structure in mouse PrP^{SC} before and after 48 hours incubation with β-breaker.

	Proportions of secondary structure (%)	
Secondary structure	*Before incubation*	*After incubation*
α-helix	18	27
β-sheet	36	9

Table 2: Time to onset of symptoms for mice treated with PrP^{SC} with and without β-breaker.

	Time to onset of symptoms (days)	
PrP^{SC} concentration (relative to stock solution)	*PrP^{SC}*	*PrP^{SC} + β-breaker*
1×10^{-2}	129	143
1×10^{-3}	145	159
1×10^{-4}	173	185

[Question 1 continues on *Page twelve*

Marks

Question 1 (continued)

(*a*) PrP^{C} and PrP^{SC} are both glycoproteins.

(i) Apart from a polypeptide, what is the other chemical component of glycoprotein? **1**

(ii) State the function of cell membrane glycoproteins. **1**

(*b*) (i) PrP^{C} and PrP^{SC} have the same primary structure. Why should they be expected to fold in an identical way? **1**

(ii) Hydrogen bonds are important in the development of secondary structure of proteins.
Name **two** other types of interactions involved in protein folding. **1**

(*c*) Refer to the data in the Figure.

(i) What evidence is there to suggest that the experimenters tested only one sample in each of the controls? **1**

(ii) Draw **two** conclusions about the effect of β-breaker on human and mouse PrP^{SC}. **2**

(*d*) Refer to the information in Table 1.

(i) Explain why the PrP^{SC} protein should be more susceptible to breakdown by intracellular enzymes after incubation. **2**

(ii) What additional information about PrP^{SC} would be required to establish if β-breaker has caused the PrP^{SC} to become fully susceptible to breakdown? **1**

(iii) Which type of enzyme would break down PrP? **1**

(*e*) Refer to the information in Table 2.

(i) At what concentration of PrP^{SC} does the β-breaker have the greatest effect? **1**

(ii) What is the effect of changing the concentration of PrP^{SC} on the onset of brain disease in mice? **1**

(*f*) Taking all the data into consideration, suggest **two** modifications to the treatments in the second study that may delay the onset of symptoms further. **2**

(15)

[Questions 2, 3 and 4 are on fold-out *Page thirteen*

Marks

2. The disaccharides maltose and trehalose each consist of two glucose molecules. Maltose is formed naturally when starch is broken down in barley grains and trehalose is an important constituent in the fluid that bathes the organs of insects. In both substances the glucose molecules are joined by a glycosidic bond. For ease of reference the glucose molecules in the diagrams are labelled a, b, c and d.

Maltose **Trehalose**

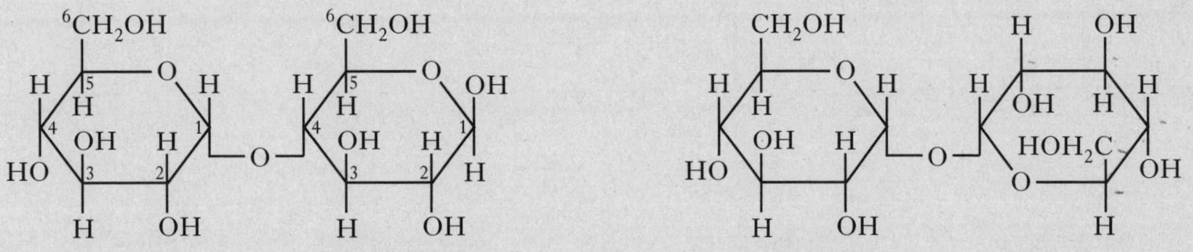

glucose a glucose b glucose c glucose d

(*a*) (i) Explain why the bond between the glucose molecules in maltose is described as alpha (1, 4). 1

(ii) In what way is the glycosidic bond different in trehalose? 1

(*b*) What type of chemical reaction is required to break a glycosidic bond? 1

(3)

3. Sickle cell anaemia is an inherited condition affecting haemoglobin. Four polypeptide chains interact to form a haemoglobin molecule. Two of the chains are designated α chains and the other two are referred to as β chains. Sickle cell anaemia arises from a mutation in the gene for β chains.
The restriction enzyme *Mst*II is able to recognise and cut DNA that has the sequence CCTNAGG, where N is any nucleotide. One of these *recognition sites*, CCTGAGG, lies within the β chain gene. In sickle cell anaemia the mutation has changed the sequence to CCTG**T**GG. This alteration to the gene can be used to screen for sickle cell anaemia.

(*a*) What type of enzyme is a restriction enzyme? 1

(*b*) Following the extraction of the DNA for the β chain of haemoglobin and its digestion with *Mst*II, what technique is used to separate the fragments produced? 1

(*c*) A probe has been designed to hybridise with the gene for the β chain. Describe the features of the probe that allow it to hybridise. 2

(*d*) (i) What is meant by a *screening test* for a disorder? 1

(ii) Explain why the action of *Mst*II allows it to be used to screen for sickle cell anaemia. 1

(6)

4. Describe how the cell cycle is controlled. **(5)**

Marks

5. The diagram shows a food web in a marine ecosystem and the vertical distribution of the organisms involved.

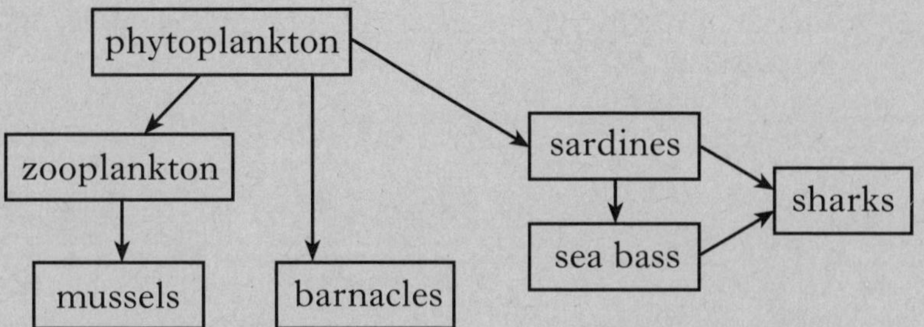

(*a*) Explain why phytoplankton are only found in the surface waters. **2**

(*b*) Within this food web there is variation in the number of trophic levels for the different food chains. Explain why a food chain rarely contains more than four trophic levels. **1**

(*c*) The diagram below shows a pyramid of biomass for the trophic levels involving phytoplankton, zooplankton and mussels in a sample from the ecosystem.

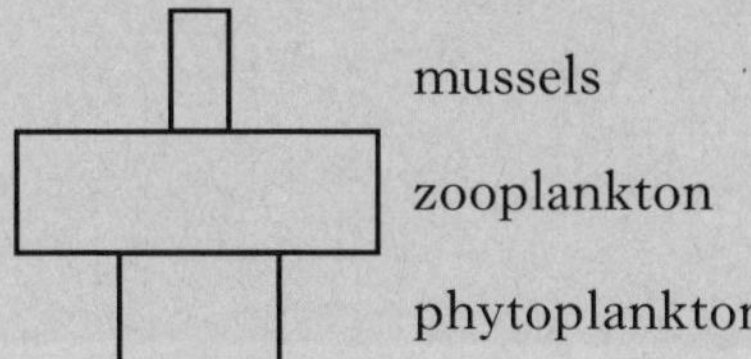

Describe how a pyramid of productivity would differ from the pyramid of biomass shown. Give one reason for the difference. **2**

(5)

Marks

6. Fur seals spend most of their lives feeding in Antarctic seas. During the short summer they come ashore to breed.

(*a*) The figure below shows the number of fur seals breeding on Signy Island from 1956 to 1986.

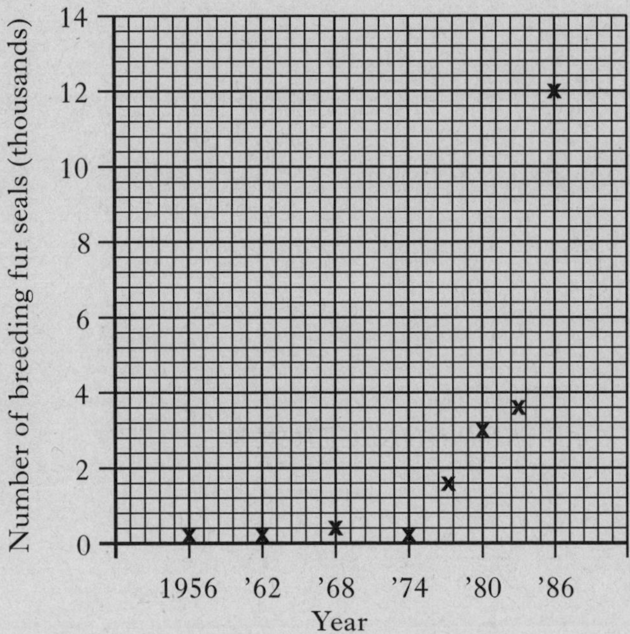

Calculate the mean annual growth rate of the seal population over the period 1980 to 1986. **1**

(*b*) Permanent quadrats were established to investigate the effect of seals on ground cover plants. The charts show the mean percentage cover of a number of plants in the permanent quadrats in 1965 and in 1985.

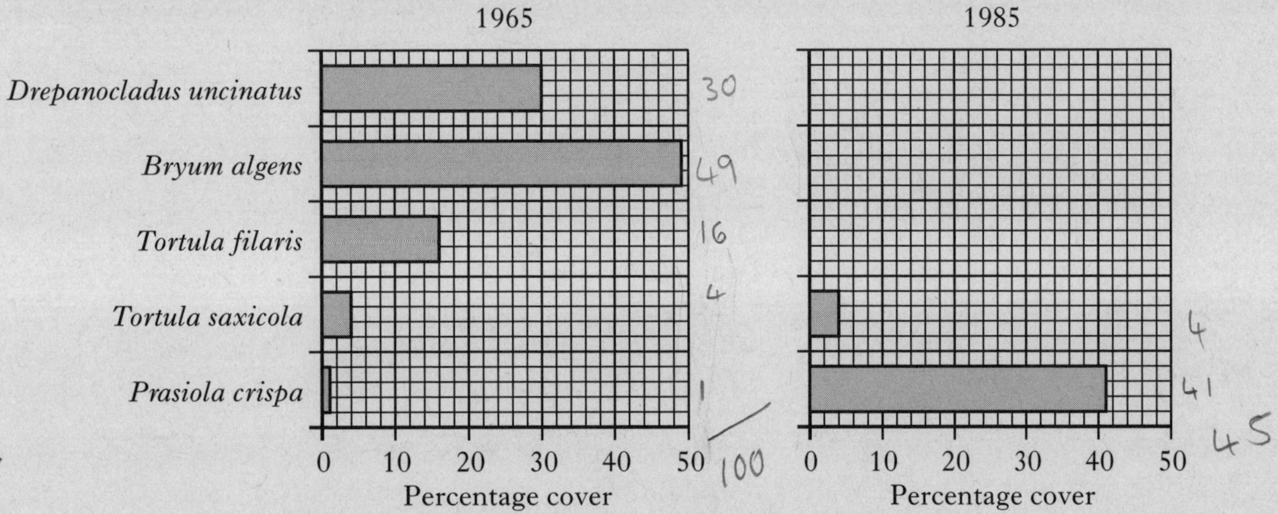

(i) What proportion of ground cover has been lost? **1**

(ii) Suggest an explanation for the disappearance of some ground cover plant species. **2**

(iii) Suggest a possible reason for the increase in percentage cover by *Prasiola crispa* during the period of the study. **1**

(*c*) Fur seals are homeothermic. Explain how this feature allows the species to survive the large temperature differences between sea and land in the Antarctic. **1**

(6)

Marks

7. Answer **either** A **or** B.

A. Give an account of ecosystem change under the following headings:

(i) main features of a primary autogenic succession; **9**

(ii) effects of human activity. **6**

(15)

OR

B. Discuss positive/negative (+/–) interactions between species under the following headings:

(i) grazing; **4**

(ii) parasitism; **5**

(iii) defence against predation. **6**

(15)

[*END OF SECTION B*]

SECTION C

Candidates should attempt questions on one unit, either Biotechnology or Animal Behaviour or Physiology, Health and Exercise.

The questions on Animal Behaviour can be found on pages 19–21.

The questions on Physiology, Health and Exercise can be found on pages 22–24.

All answers must be written clearly and legibly in ink.

Labelled diagrams may be used where appropriate.

Marks

Biotechnology

1. To create *Flavr Savr* tomatoes, a gene from the original tomato is cloned, engineered and re-introduced into the tomato cells so that both genes are present in the same cells. The diagram shows the transcription of both genes.

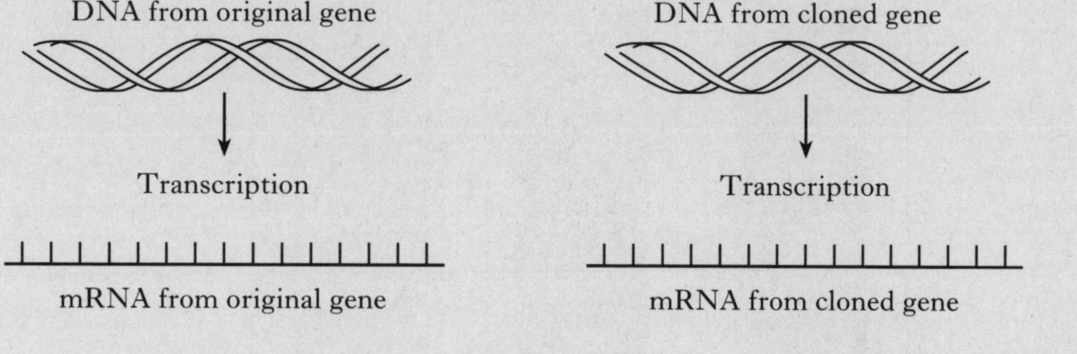

(*a*) Explain why, in *Flavr Savr* tomatoes, no protein will be formed from the original gene. **2**

(*b*) (i) Which protein is **not** produced as a result of this modification? **1**

(ii) Give one commercial advantage of producing tomatoes this way. **1**

(*c*) *Flavr Savr* tomatoes were tested and found to be safe. Why then was there consumer resistance to buying them? **1**

(5)

2. The diagram shows steps involved in producing monoclonal antibodies.

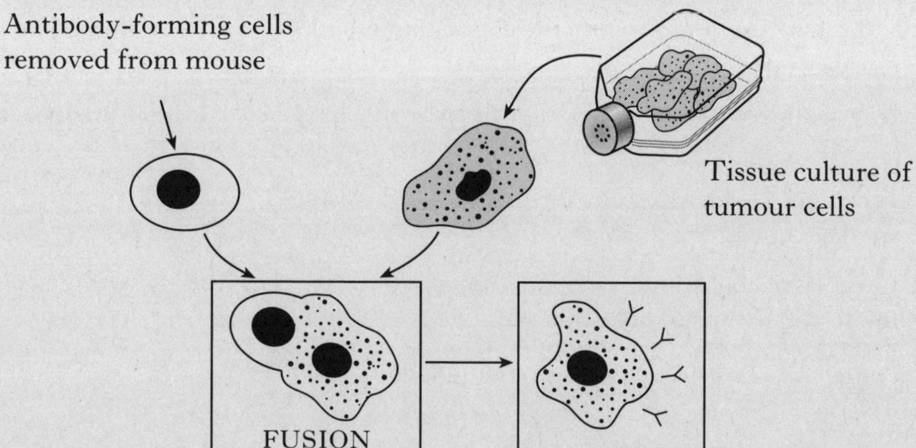

(*a*) Which cell type in the mouse produces antibodies? **1**

(*b*) Why are the antibody-forming cells fused with tumour cells? **1**

(*c*) What term is used to describe the fused cells? **1**

(*d*) The tumour cells selected for fusion have lost their ability to synthesise antibody molecules. Why is this important? **1**

 (4)

Biotechnology **(continued)** *Marks*

3. Discuss the role of enzymes in the commercial production of fruit juices. **(4)**

4. Grass is converted to silage to provide winter feed for cattle. The aim of the ensilage process is to conserve the high nutritional value of grass. The figure below shows the distribution of nitrogen-containing compounds in grass, good silage and poor silage.

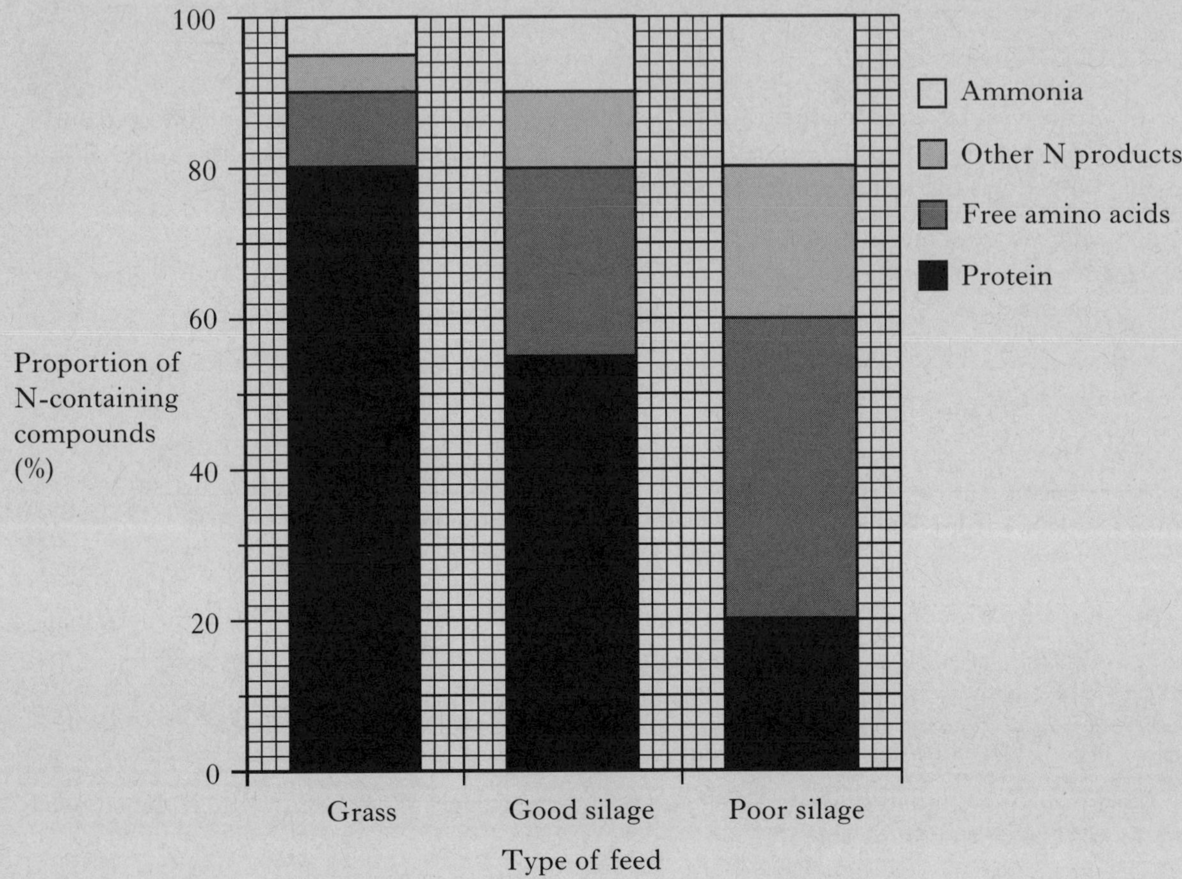

(*a*) Use the data to describe how good silage differs from grass. 2

(*b*) Express the free amino acid content of grass, good silage and poor silage as a simple whole number ratio. 1

(*c*) The farmer believes that spoilage micro-organisms have caused the formation of poor silage.

(i) From the evidence, what changes have resulted from the activity of the spoilage micro-organisms? 2

(ii) Give **two** conditions that are required to prevent the growth of spoilage micro-organisms in good silage. 1

(iii) Name a bacterium involved in making good silage. 1

(7)

(20)

[End of *Biotechnology* questions. *Animal Behaviour* questions start on Page 19]

SECTION C (continued)

Marks

Animal Behaviour

1. Wild chimpanzees are frugivores, feeding principally on sugar-rich fruit. However, they frequently hunt in groups and share meat obtained from prey such as red colobus monkeys. The groups may hunt between 4–10 times each month.

Three hypotheses have been formulated to explain chimpanzee hunting behaviour.

Hypothesis 1 — Nutritional shortfall
This suggests that chimpanzees hunt to compensate for seasonal shortages in food availability. Figure 1 shows the relationship between hunting frequency and the availability of fruit.

Hypothesis 2 — Reproductive success
This argues that male chimpanzees hunt to obtain meat that they exchange for matings with females. Figure 2 shows the relationship between meat sharing and successful approaches for mating. The error bars represent the standard error, which is a measure of the variation in the samples.

Hypothesis 3 — Male bonding
This proposes that males use meat as a social tool to develop and maintain alliances with other males.

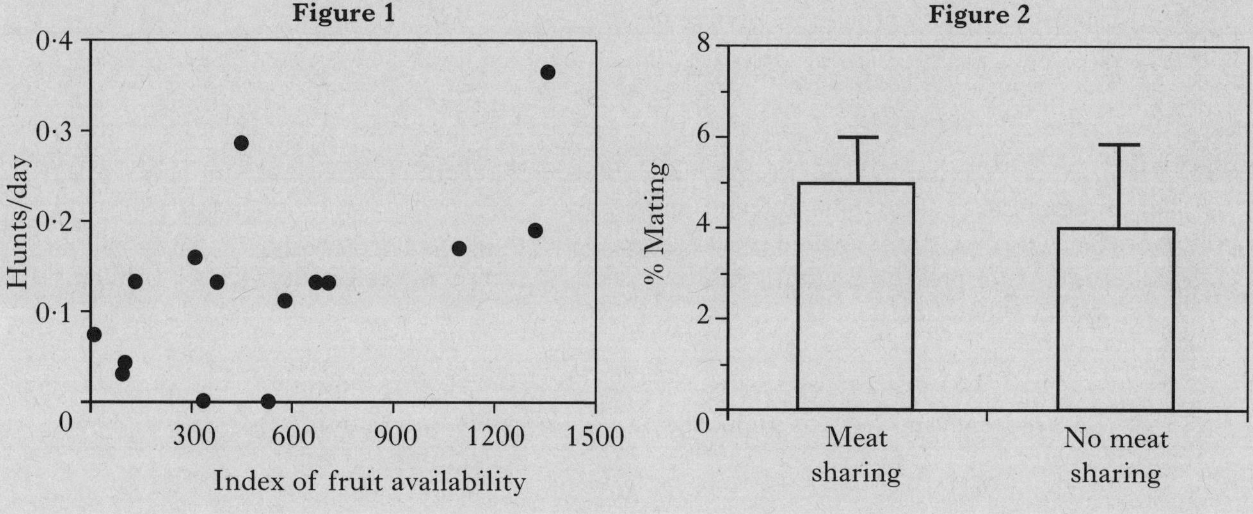

(*a*) How could the data shown in Figures 1 and 2 be used to reject Hypotheses 1 and 2? **2**

(*b*) If Hypothesis 3 was correct, suggest one example of behaviour that a researcher might observe. **1**

(*c*) Describe the main features of social hierarchies found in primate groups such as chimpanzees. **5**

(8)

[Turn over

Animal Behaviour **(continued)** *Marks*

2. Dispersal and predation have been studied in an Iberian lynx population in south western Spain. The table below shows some differences between Iberian lynxes and African lions.

Feature	*Iberian lynxes*	*African lions*
Mating system	Monogamy	Polygamy
Natal dispersal	Males and females	Mainly males
Ultimate cause of dispersal	Competition for mates or territories	Avoidance of inbreeding
Hunting strategy	Solitary	Co-operative

(*a*) Explain why it is important for animals to avoid inbreeding. 2

(*b*) Distinguish between the mating systems reported in the table. 1

(*c*) Explain what is meant by "ultimate cause" in relation to animal behaviour in general. 1

(*d*) State one benefit of co-operative hunting. 1

(5)

3. Habituation is a simple behaviour in which there is a progressive decrease in the response of an animal to a continuous or repeated stimulus. In a recent study of habituation and courtship in the three-spined stickleback, *Gasterosteus aculeatus*, males in breeding condition were presented with a choice of two dummy females displaying two different postures as illustrated below.

Head-up dummy
(representing receptive female)

Horizontal dummy
(representing normally swimming female)

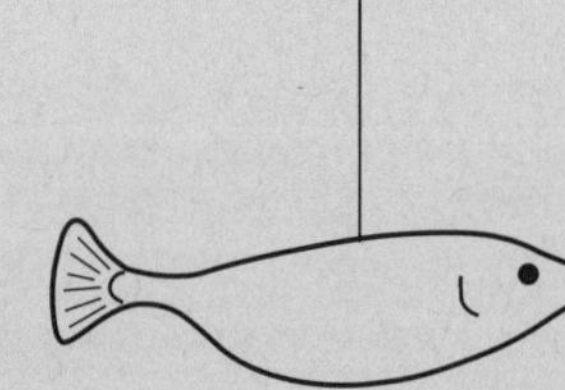

The behaviour of males was recorded on videotape for 1 hour after simultaneous presentation of both dummies. In particular, the number of zigzag displays performed and the number of bites were counted. The results are shown in the Figures (a) and (b) opposite.

Animal Behaviour **Question 3 (continued)** *Marks*

Figure (a) Zigzags per 4 minute block

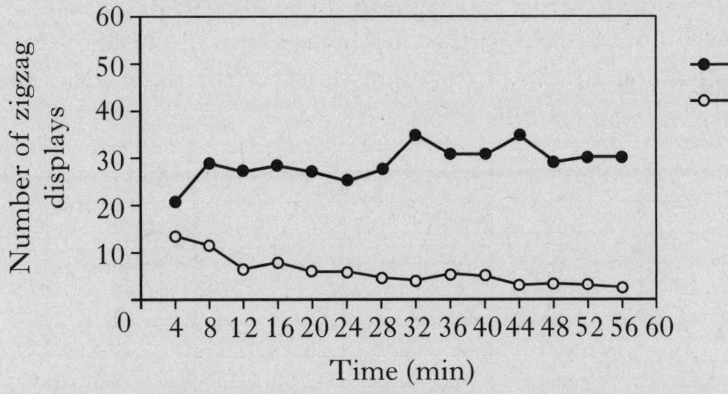

Figure (b) Bites per 4 minute block

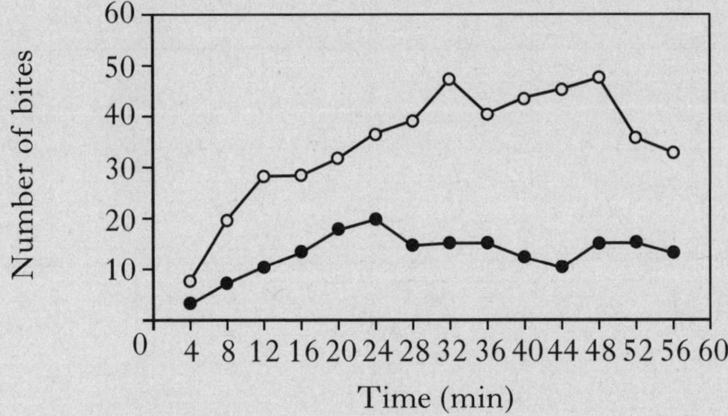

(*a*) Explain why habituation can be defined as a form of learning. **1**

(*b*) The head-up posture (stimulus) elicits the stereotyped response of zigzagging. In this example of behaviour, what term is used to describe:

(i) the stimulus;

(ii) the response? **2**

(*c*) Which of the dummies produces habituation in the zigzag response? Use the data presented to justify your answer. **1**

(*d*) To ensure validity in setting up this experiment, describe one precaution that should be taken either in relation to the dummy fish or the choice of sticklebacks. **1**

(*e*) Suggest why the stickleback behaviour in this experiment was videotaped. **1**

(*f*) Suggest an anthropomorphic explanation for the results shown in Figure (b). **1**

(7)

(20)

[End of *Animal Behaviour* questions. *Physiology, Health and Exercise* questions start on Page 22]

SECTION C (continued)

Marks

Physiology, Health and Exercise

1. The figure below shows the printout from the heart rate monitor of a 30 year old cyclist completing a time trial. The time trial is a race against the clock over a distance of 36 km on an out-and-back course where all the competitors start and finish at the same place returning from the half way point by the reverse route.

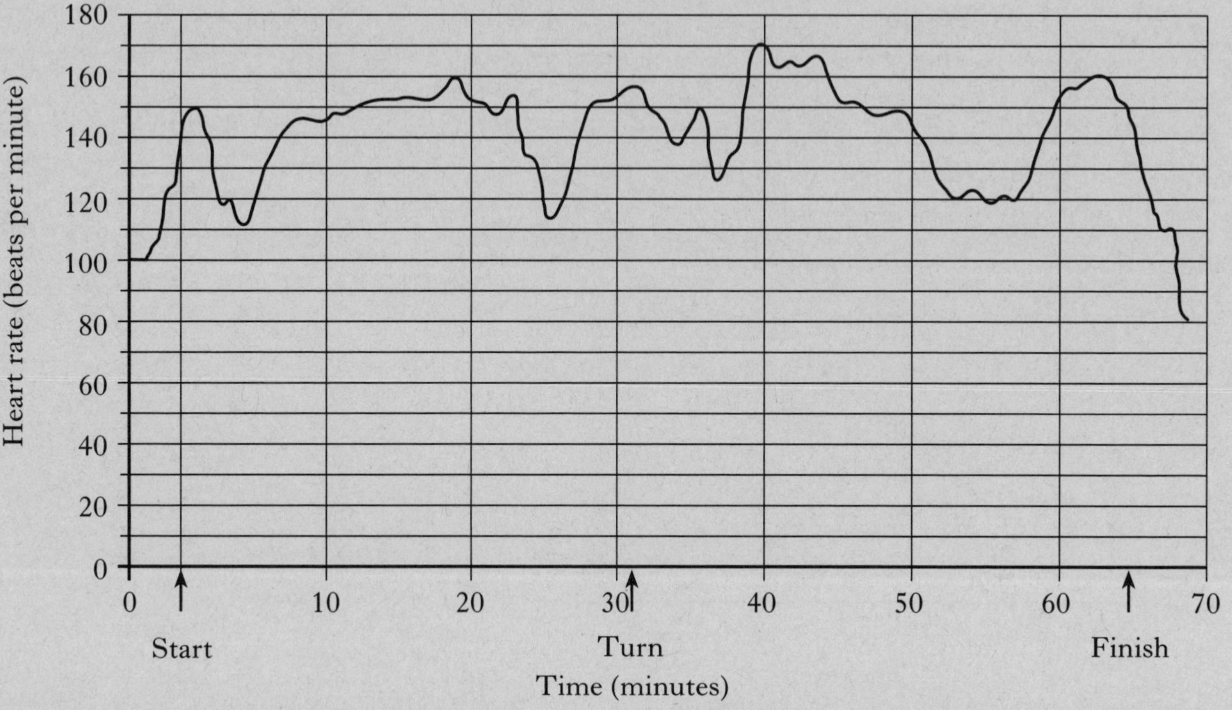

(*a*) What changes to the distribution of blood would have occurred in the cyclist's body as he began the race? **1**

(*b*) The cyclist is a trained athlete. How would the structure of his heart differ from that of an untrained individual? **1**

(*c*) What **two** pieces of evidence from the figure suggest that the cyclist "warmed up" before the race? **2**

(*d*) An estimate of maximal heart rate, in beats per minute, can be determined by subtracting the person's age in years from 220. What is the highest percentage of this cyclist's maximal heart rate reached during the race? **1**

(*e*) After the race the cyclist said, "I was feeling really good on the way out but my legs felt like lead on the way back". Suggest **two** reasons for the difference between the out and return journeys. **2**

(*f*) Give **two** differences in the results that would be expected if an untrained person was monitored while cycling the same course. **2**

(9)

Physiology, Health and Exercise **(continued)** *Marks*

2. The following figure shows the results of a glucose tolerance test for two subjects A and B. Each fasted for a period of twelve hours and was then given 50 g glucose in a 150 cm^3 drink. Blood glucose levels were then monitored for 3 hours.

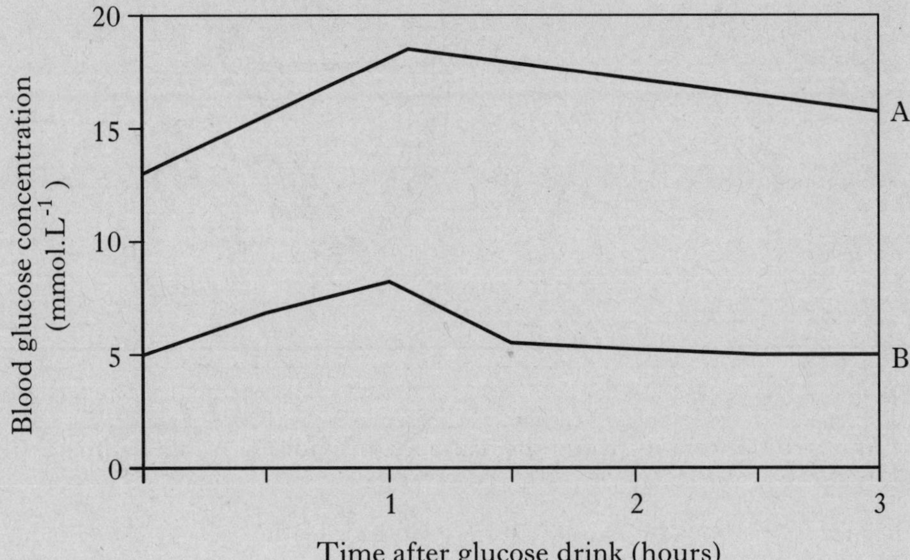

(*a*) Subject B has normal control of blood glucose. Give **two** pieces of evidence from the data that suggest subject A is diabetic. 2

(*b*) Give **two** effects of insulin that would give rise to the response shown after one hour in subject B. 1

(3)

[Turn over for Questions 3 and 4 on *Page twenty four*

Physiology, Health and Exercise **(continued)** *Marks*

3. The illustration below shows calipers used to estimate percentage body fat.

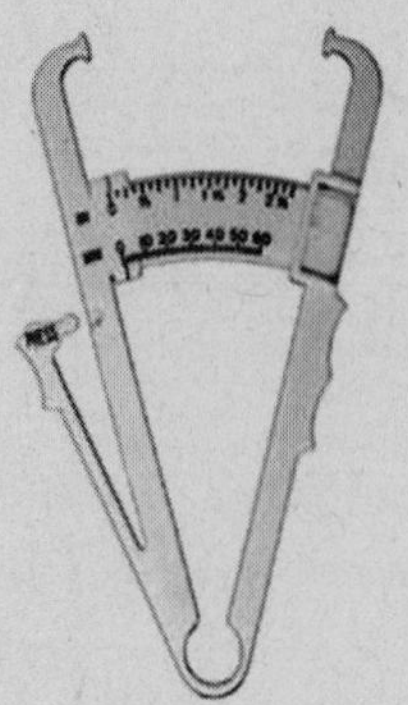

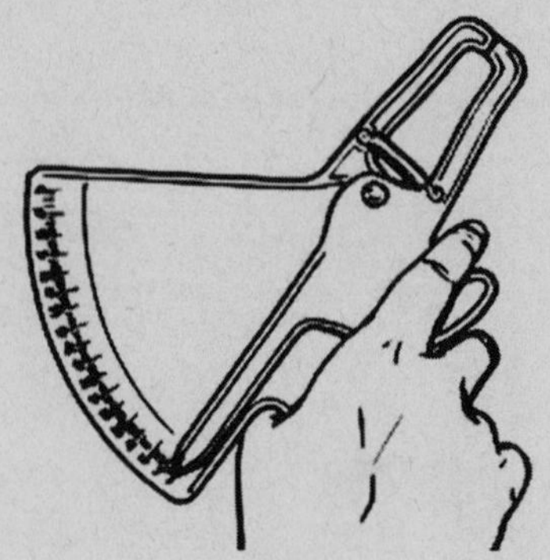

(*a*) What does the device measure? **1**

(*b*) Explain how the procedure for using the calipers provides a valid estimate of percentage body fat. **2**

(*c*) Name **two** alternative methods of estimating percentage body fat. **1**

(4)

4. Describe how some of the factors that contribute to cardiovascular disease can be modified to reduce the risk. **(4)**

(20)

[*END OF QUESTION PAPER*]

ADVANCED HIGHER

2007

[BLANK PAGE]

X007/701

NATIONAL QUALIFICATIONS 2007

MONDAY, 21 MAY
1.00 PM – 3.30 PM

BIOLOGY
ADVANCED HIGHER

SECTION A—Questions 1–25 (25 marks)

Instructions for completion of Section A are given on *Page two*.

SECTIONS B AND C

The answer to each question should be written in ink in the answer book provided. Any additional paper (if used) should be placed inside the front cover of the answer book.

Rough work should be scored through.

Section B (55 marks)

All questions should be attempted. Candidates should note that Question 8 contains a choice.

Question 1 is on Pages 8, 9 and 10. Questions 2, 3 and 4 are on Page 11. Pages 10 and 11 are fold-out pages.

Section C (20 marks)

Candidates should attempt the questions in **one** unit, **either** Biotechnology **or** Animal Behaviour **or** Physiology, Health and Exercise.

Read carefully

1 Check that the answer sheet provided is for **Biology Advanced Higher (Section A)**.

2 For this section of the examination you must use an **HB pencil** and, where necessary, an eraser.

3 Check that the answer sheet you have been given has **your name**, **date of birth**, **SCN** (Scottish Candidate Number) and **Centre Name** printed on it.

Do not change any of these details.

4 If any of this information is wrong, tell the Invigilator immediately.

5 If this information is correct, **print** your name and seat number in the boxes provided.

6 The answer to each question is **either** A, B, C or D. Decide what your answer is, then, using your pencil, put a horizontal line in the space provided (see sample question below).

7 There is **only one correct** answer to each question.

8 Any rough working should be done on the question paper or the rough working sheet, **not** on your answer sheet.

9 At the end of the exam, put the **answer sheet for Section A inside the front cover of the answer book**.

Sample Question

Which of the following molecules contains six carbon atoms?

A Glucose

B Pyruvic acid

C Ribulose bisphosphate

D Acetyl coenzyme A

The correct answer is **A**—Glucose. The answer **A** has been clearly marked in **pencil** with a horizontal line (see below).

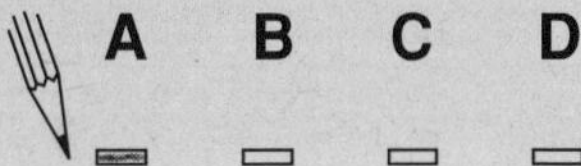

Changing an answer

If you decide to change your answer, carefully erase your first answer and using your pencil, fill in the answer you want. The answer below has been changed to **D**.

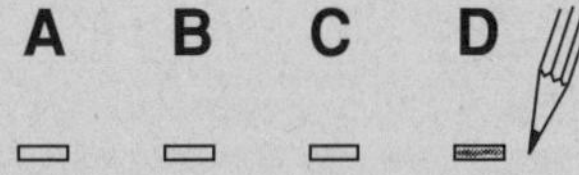

SECTION A

All questions in this section should be attempted.

Answers should be given on the separate answer sheet provided.

1. What name is given to the cytoplasmic connections that link adjacent plant cells?

A Microvilli

B Microfilaments

C Plasmodesmata

D Middle lamellae

2. The figure below shows the number of cells in a tissue sample at various stages of the cell cycle.

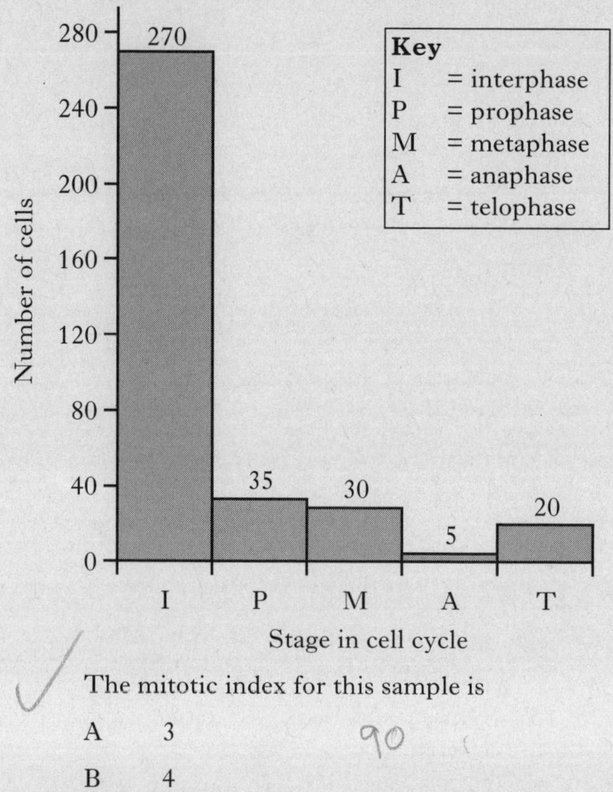

The mitotic index for this sample is

A 3

B 4

C 25

D 33.

3. Which line in the table correctly describes the chemical reaction in which a fatty acid is joined to a glycerol?

	Type of reaction	*Type of bond formed*
A	hydrolysis	ester
B	condensation	glycosidic
C	hydrolysis	glycosidic
D	condensation	ester

4. Which of the following diagrams illustrates a peptide bond?

A $-\overset{\overset{\large O}{\|}}{C}-\underset{\underset{\large H}{|}}{N}-$

B $-\underset{\underset{H\ \ H}{\underset{/\ \backslash}{N}}}{\underset{|}{C}}=\overset{\overset{H}{|}}{C}-$

C $-\underset{\underset{H}{|}}{\overset{\overset{H}{|}}{C}}-\underset{\underset{\underset{H}{|}}{N}}{\overset{}{\underset{\|}{C}}}-$

D $-\underset{\underset{H\ \ H}{\underset{/\ \backslash}{N}}}{\underset{|}{\overset{\overset{H}{|}}{C}}}-\underset{\underset{H}{|}}{\overset{\overset{H}{|}}{C}}-$

5. The proportion of sugars produced in the breakdown of starch can be measured by the dextrose equivalent (DE). The DE can be calculated as follows:

$$DE = 100 \times \frac{\text{number of glycosidic bonds broken}}{\text{number of glycosidic bonds originally present}}$$

What is the approximate DE when an amylose molecule is completely digested to maltose?

A 0·5

B 1·0

C 50

D 100

6. Which of the following describes the structure of cytosine?

A A purine base with a single-ring structure

B A purine base with a double-ring structure

C A pyrimidine base with a single-ring structure

D A pyrimidine base with a double-ring structure

[Turn over

7. A diploid cell contains 6×10^9 base pairs of genetic code. Only 4% of this codes for protein.

How many anticodons does this represent?

A $2{\cdot}4 \times 10^7$

B 8×10^7

C $2{\cdot}4 \times 10^8$

D 8×10^8

8. To which group of signalling molecules does testosterone belong?

A Extracellular hydrophobic

B Extracellular hydrophilic

C Peptide hormone

D Neurotransmitter

9. Enzymes that catalyse the hydrolysis of phosphodiester bonds in genetic material are called

A kinases

B ligases

C ATPases

D nucleases.

10. The diagram below shows the effect of isoleucine on the enzyme threonine deaminase.

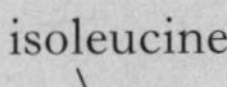

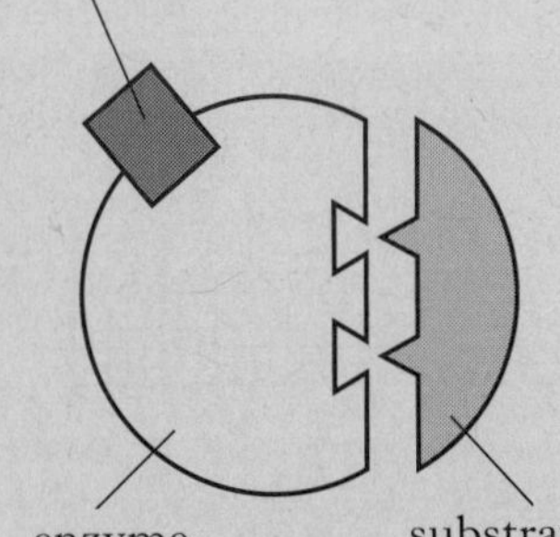

enzyme substrate

isoleucine present

isoleucine absent

In high concentrations, isoleucine acts as

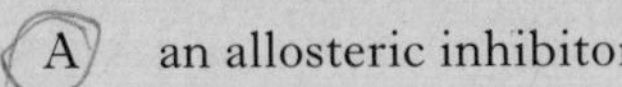

A an allosteric inhibitor

B an allosteric activator

C a competitive inhibitor

D a positive modulator.

11. The graph shows the results of an investigation using the enzyme invertase that breaks down sucrose into glucose and fructose. 1 g of sucrose was dissolved in $100\,cm^3$ water and $2\,cm^3$ of a 1% invertase solution was added.

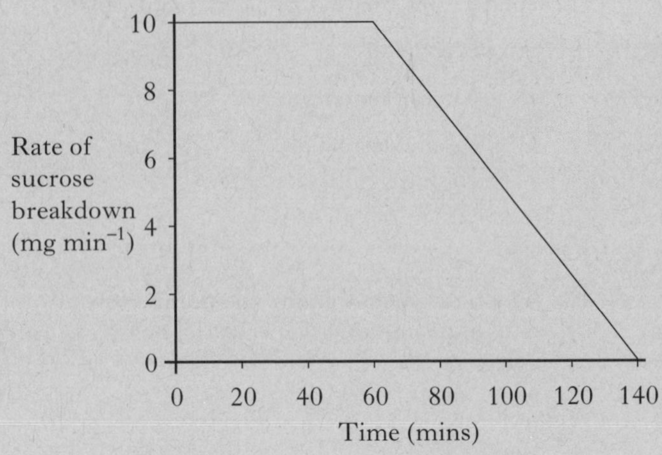

Which of the following conclusions can be drawn from this information?

A At 70 minutes exactly half the substrate remains.

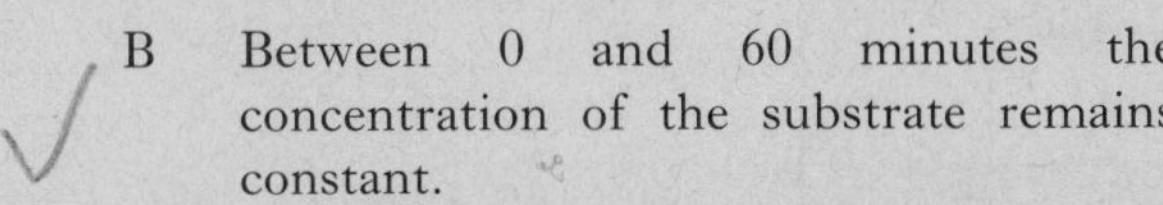

B Between 0 and 60 minutes the concentration of the substrate remains constant.

C At 140 minutes the enzyme is no longer active.

D Between 60 and 140 minutes the concentration of the substrate is the limiting factor.

12. The following stages are used to introduce a "foreign" gene into a tomato plant.

W Descendent plant cells receive copies of foreign gene.

X Foreign gene inserted into plasmid.

Y Altered plasmid introduced into cultured plant cells.

Z Plasmid isolated from *Agrobacterium tumefaciens*.

These stages would occur in the order

A Y, W, X, Z

B Z, X, Y, W

C X, Z, W, Y

D Z, Y, X, W.

13. Which of the following processes only takes place in autotrophs?

A Assimilation

B Decomposition

C Photosynthesis

D Respiration

14. The number of trophic levels in a food chain is limited because at each level the

A amount of energy decreases

B number of organisms decreases

C biomass decreases

D productivity decreases.

15. In aquatic ecosystems the amount of sunlight absorbed by water increases with depth.

Absorption by seawater is greater than absorption by fresh water.

Which of the following graphs represents the relationship between depth and light intensity in fresh water and seawater?

Key

——— fresh water

--------- seawater

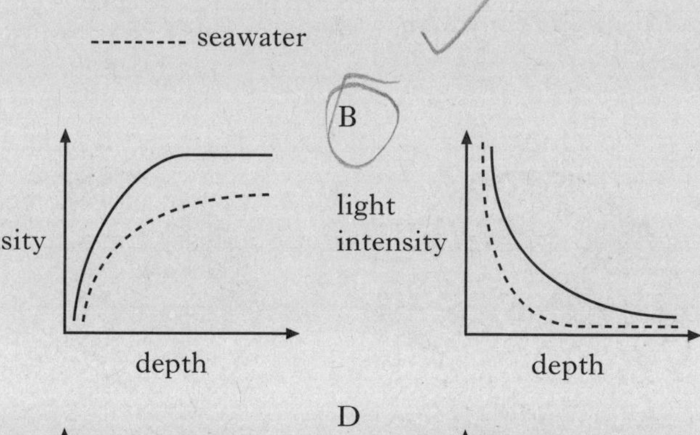

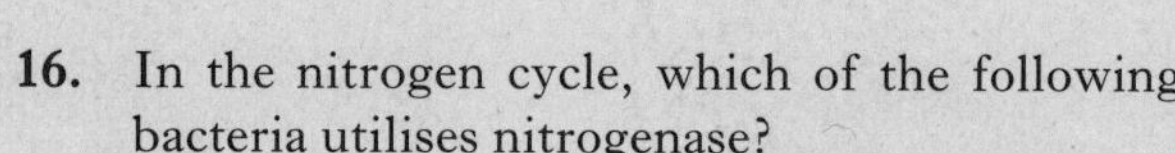

16. In the nitrogen cycle, which of the following bacteria utilises nitrogenase?

A *Rhizobium*

B *Nitrosomonas*

C *Nitrobacter*

D *Pseudomonas*

17. A flask was set up to demonstrate the activity of some of the micro-organisms involved in the nitrogen cycle. The concentration of nitrite in the solution was measured over several weeks and the results are shown in the graph.

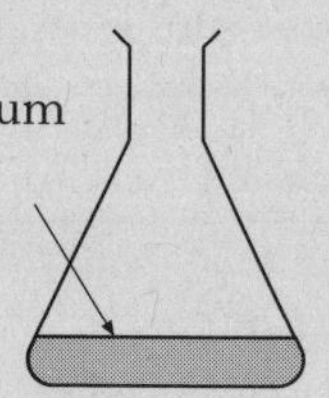

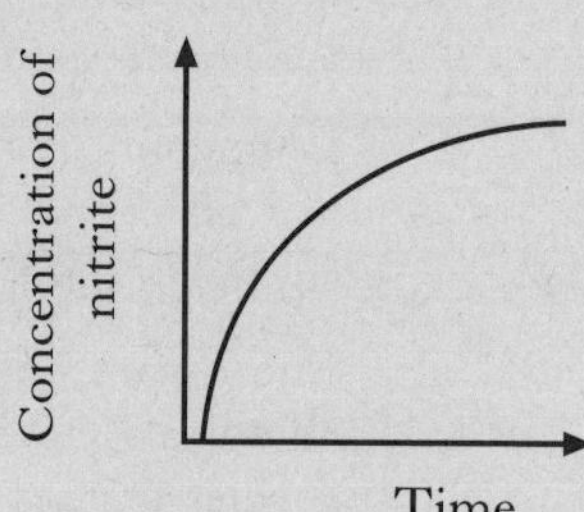

Which process has been shown to be taking place in the flask?

A Ammonification

B Nitrification

C Nitrogen fixation

D Denitrification

18. The graph shows the effect of adding different amounts of fertiliser on the yield of a crop plant.

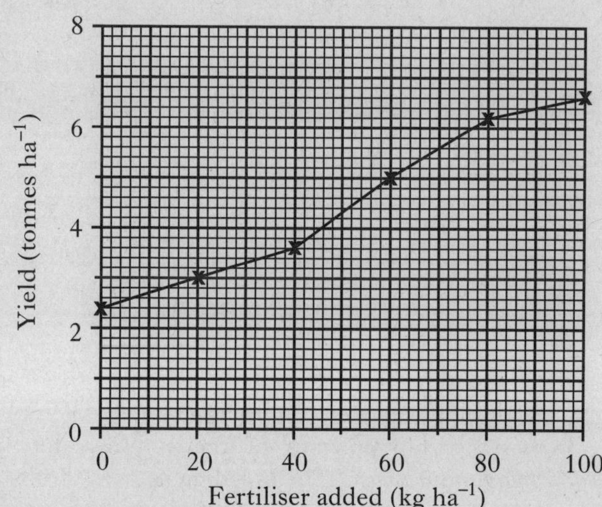

The percentage increase in yield obtained when the fertiliser is increased from 40 to 80 kg ha^{-1} is

A 26

B 40

C 58

D 72.

[Turn over

19. Which of the following is an example of *exploitation* competition?

A Red grouse, through aggressive behaviour, establish a territory which provides food and cover.

B A population of moose living on an island share a limited supply of food.

C Dandelions have evolved a flat rosette leaf arrangement which maximises their supply of light.

D Encrusting sponges use poisonous chemicals to overcome other sponge species as they expand to fill open space on rock surfaces.

20. Which of the graphs best represents the relationship between the intensity of rabbit grazing and the diversity of plant species in a series of grassland plots?

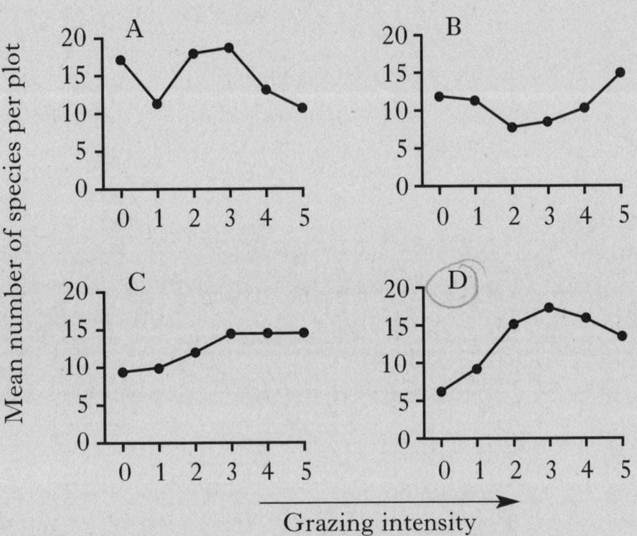

21. The piping plover (*Charadrius melodus*) often nests within colonies of the common tern (*Sterna hirundo*). The breeding success of the plover is greater when nesting takes place within a tern colony. The breeding success of terns is very similar in colonies with and without plovers. This suggests that the relationship between the two species is

A commensalism

B mutualism

C parasitism

D competitive.

22. The table shows some of the characteristics of a number of agricultural fertilisers.

	Fertiliser			
Characteristic	*A*	*B*	*C*	*D*
Phosphate concentration	high	high	low	high
Nitrate concentration	high	low	high	high
Nutrient release rate	slow	slow	fast	fast

Which of these fertilisers would be most likely to cause eutrophication in an aquatic ecosystem?

23. Soils are mixtures of rock particles of different sizes called clay, silt and sand. The table shows the composition of a number of different soil types.

	Particle size (%)		
Soil type	*Clay*	*Silt*	*Sand*
sandy clay loam	20 – 30	0 – 30	50 – 80
clay loam	20 – 35	20 – 60	20 – 50
sandy silt loam	0 – 20	40 – 80	20 – 50
silty clay loam	20 – 35	45 – 80	0 – 20

Which of the following represents a clay loam?

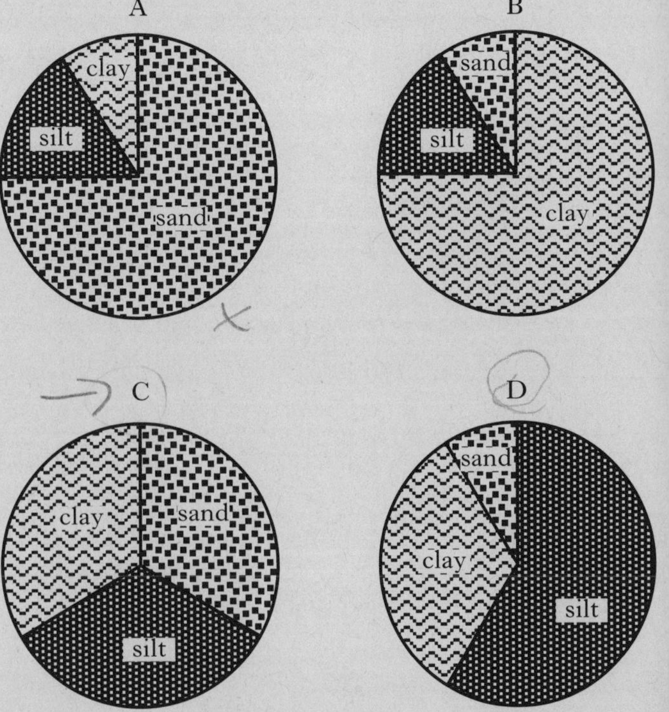

24. The following gases can all be atmospheric pollutants.

1 Carbon dioxide

2 Methane

3 Nitrous oxide

4 Sulphur dioxide

Those that contribute to the formation of acid rain are

A 1, 2, 3 and 4

B 1, 3 and 4 only

C 1, 2 and 4 only

D 3 and 4 only.

25. The figure shows the concentration of dieldrin (a pesticide) in an alga, the water flea *Daphnia* and a small fish known as a guppy. The species were immersed separately in a solution of dieldrin. The *Daphnia* were not fed during the test; the fish were fed on uncontaminated *Daphnia*.

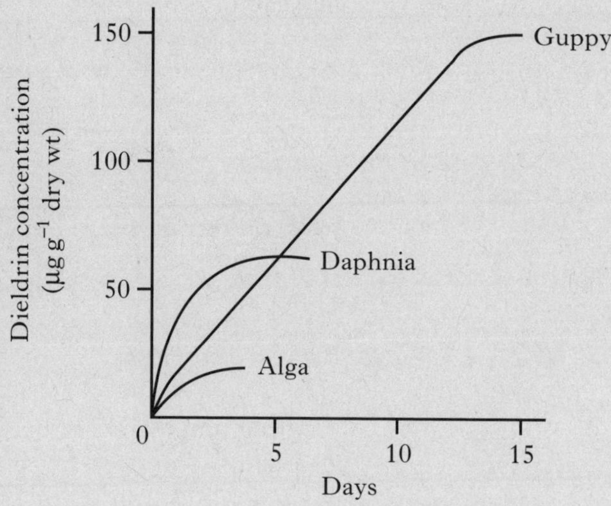

The results in the graph are a consequence of

A biological magnification

B bioaccumulation

C biotransformation

D biodegradation.

[*END OF SECTION A*]

Candidates are reminded that the answer sheet MUST be returned INSIDE the front cover of the answer book.

[Turn over for Section B on *Page eight*

SECTION B

All questions in this section should be attempted.
All answers must be written clearly and legibly in ink.

1. The Asian musk shrew (*Suncus murinus*), an efficient and rapid coloniser originating in India, has reached the island of Mauritius. The shrew is frequently transported unknowingly in ships' cargoes and personal baggage. It is responsible for a number of damaging ecological effects and is fast becoming a pest species of global proportions, especially in small island ecosystems.

Figure 1: The Asian musk shrew (*Suncus murinus*)

One conservation programme to eradicate the shrew has been attempted on Ile aux Aigrettes, a small island nature reserve off the coast of Mauritius. In the programme, "live" traps were used with a trap-door mechanism closing behind any animal entering. Traps were checked daily and any shrews caught were killed; other species were released unharmed.

The locations for traps were marked out on a grid to give 1650 potential trapping points covering the whole island. Trapping started in August 1999 at the western end of the island. At intervals of 6 to 15 days, traps were moved progressively across the island until all points had been covered. Five more trapping "sweeps" were carried out to give six in total. Trapping results are shown in Table 1; these are reported as *trap nights*, values obtained by multiplying the number of traps used by the number of nights the sweeps lasted.

The shrew's breeding period lasts from November to March. Pregnant females were only found in traps from late November to January.

Each location was classified according to the four main vegetation types found on the island. The percentage cover of vegetation types is shown in Table 2. Observed and expected capture data in these four vegetation types are shown in Figure 2.

Table 1: Capture rates of shrews during each trapping sweep

Sweep number	*Dates (1999–2000)*	*Number of trap nights*	*Capture rate (Number of shrews per 10 000 trap nights)*
1	Early August	12 804	589
2	Late August	16 569	15
3	Early September	10 080	2
4	Late September	9 669	2
5	October–November	22 751	11
6	December–January	24 740	15

Question 1 (continued)

Table 2: Vegetation types on Ile aux Aigrettes

Vegetation type	*Description*	*Cover (%)*
Coastal	Native, dense scrub. No forest	31
Ebony forest	Native tree species	37
"Weeded" forest	Invasive plants removed with native species being replanted	25
Leucaena forest	Monoculture of an introduced species	7

Figure 2: Observed and expected captures in each vegetation type

The expected capture values assume that shrews are uniformly spread across the island and are not affected by vegetation type.

Total number in this capture sample is 524.

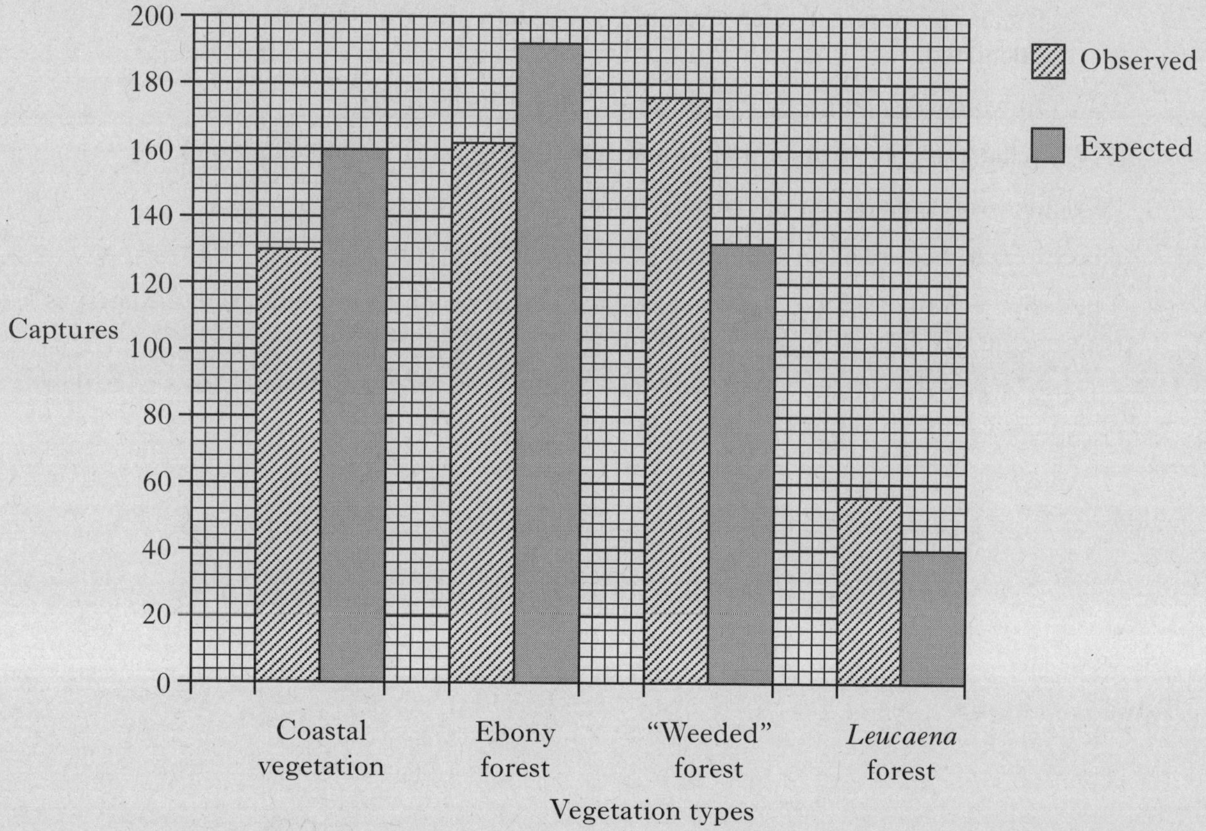

[Question 1 continues on *Page ten*

Marks

Question 1 (continued)

(*a*) (i) What term is used to describe foreign, introduced species such as the Asian musk shrew? 1

(ii) State **one** possible "damaging ecological effect" of such a species. 1

(*b*) Refer to the data in Table 1.

(i) Explain why capture rates are presented as "number of shrews per 10 000 trap nights". 1

(ii) Initially the conservation team believed the eradication programme was successful. However, by the end, they had to conclude that it had failed.

Use the data to show why they changed their minds. 2

(*c*) The conservation team concluded that it was important to trap when the shrews were not breeding. How is this conclusion justified by the information given? 1

(*d*) Refer to the data in Table 2 and Figure 2.

(i) The expected capture values are based on the assumption that the shrews are spread uniformly across the island.

Using ebony forest as an example, show how the expected capture values were calculated. 2

(ii) In which vegetation type is shrew density at its highest? 1

(iii) What evidence is there that human activity affects shrew distribution? 1

(*e*) Pesticides were considered as a means of eradicating the shrews.

Describe **one** feature of an ecologically "desirable" pesticide. 1

(*f*) The term "commensal" has been used by the conservation team to describe the shrew's relationship with humans. What is meant by the term commensal? 1

(*g*) Suggest a control measure that could be introduced, in addition to the eradication programme, to help eliminate the Asian musk shrew. 1

(13)

[Questions 2, 3 and 4 are on fold-out *Page eleven*

Marks

2. In an investigation into decomposition, discs of oak leaves were enclosed in nylon mesh bags with either large (7 mm) or small (1 mm) mesh size. The bags were then buried in garden soil. The 1 mm mesh excluded larger soil invertebrates such as earthworms and millipedes. The leaf discs were weighed at the start and thereafter at yearly intervals.

Mesh size (mm)	*Percentage of leaf disc mass remaining*		
	November 2004	*November 2005*	*November 2006*
1	100	38	30
7	100	15	8

(*a*) What term is used to describe invertebrates that feed on dead organic material? **1**

(*b*) Explain why the leaf disc mass decreased faster in 7 mm bags than in 1 mm bags. **2**

(*c*) State **one** final product of the processes taking place inside the nylon bags. **1**

(*d*) A predictable sequence of changes in community structure occurs in the bags as the organic material disappears. What term is used to describe this sequence? **1**

(5)

3. Discuss the responses of regulators to variations in the external environment. **(5)**

4. The liver fluke *Fasciola hepatica* is a parasitic flatworm. The figure shows the relationship between the mean daily egg output per adult worm and the mean number of worms present in its sheep host.

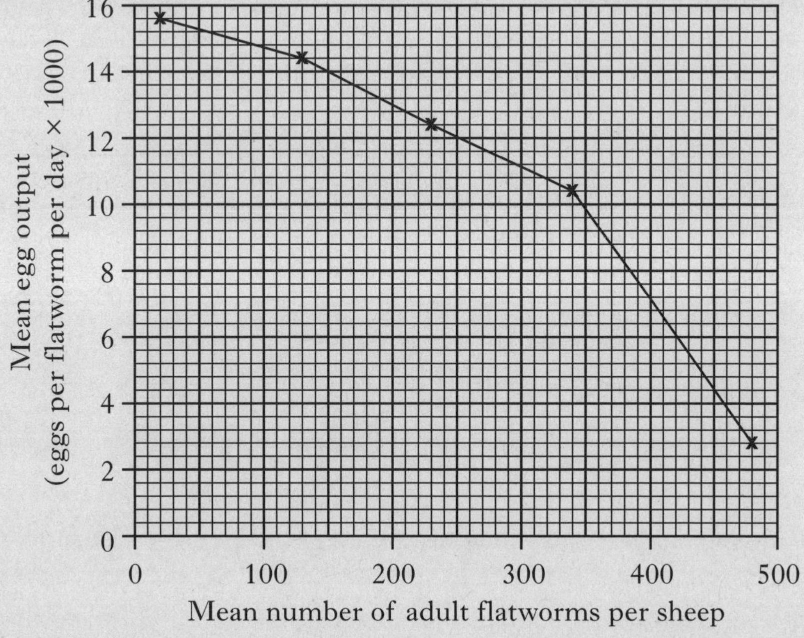

(*a*) Explain how the decreasing rate of egg production shows a density-dependent effect. **1**

(*b*) The flatworm uses a snail species as a secondary host.

Describe the role of the snail in the life cycle of the liver fluke. **1**

(*c*) Explain how the health of a sheep may affect the outcome of a fluke infestation. **1**

(*d*) Describe **one** measure that can be used to prevent infestation of a host by a parasite. **1**

(4)

Marks

5. *Retinoblastoma* is a rare cancer that develops in the eyes of children. Mutation in both copies of the retinoblastoma (*Rb*) gene results in proliferation of cells that would normally form retinal tissue. The protein arising from the *Rb* gene is abundant in the nucleus of all normal mammalian cells where it has an important role in the cell cycle.

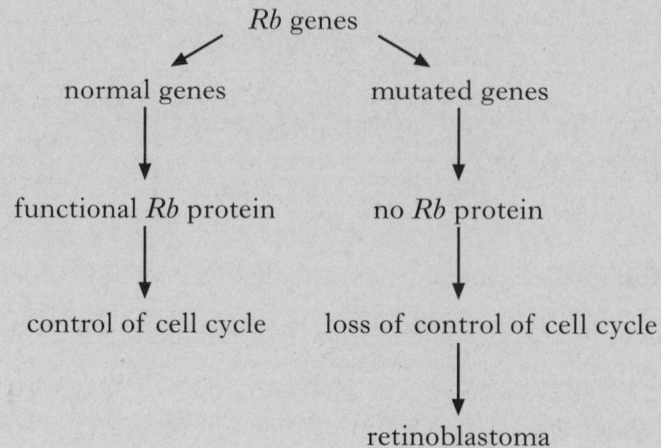

When phosphorylated, the *Rb* protein binds to gene regulatory proteins and prevents them from activating cell proliferation. When unphosphorylated, it cannot bind to the gene regulatory proteins.

(*a*) Explain why kinase enzyme activity might restrict cell division when functional *Rb* protein is abundant. **2**

(*b*) Explain how the information provided indicates that the *Rb* gene is **not** a proto-oncogene. **1**

(3)

6. *Amoeba* is a unicellular organism found in fresh water. It uses a contractile vacuole to eliminate water entering by osmosis. The data below show the concentrations of sodium ions (Na^+) and potassium ions (K^+) in the external medium, cytoplasm and contractile vacuole of *Amoeba* in culture.

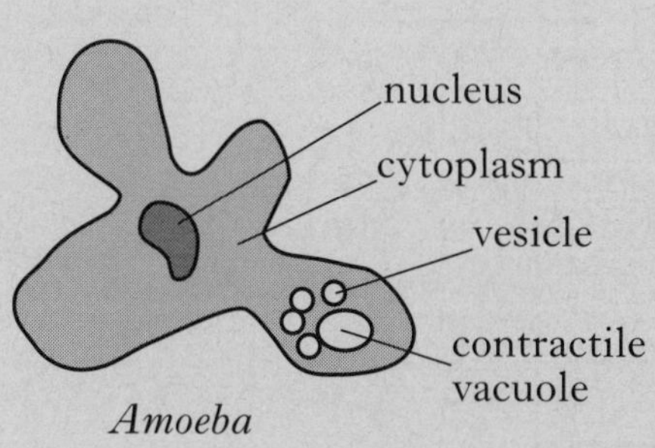

Amoeba

	Ion concentrations (mmol L^{-1})		
Ion	*External Medium*	*Cytoplasm*	*Vacuole*
sodium	0·2	0·6	19·8
potassium	0·1	31·0	4·6

(*a*) Give **two** characteristics that would distinguish prokaryotic organisms from an *Amoeba*. **1**

(*b*) Show as a whole number ratio the relative concentrations of sodium ions in the external medium, cytoplasm and vacuole. **1**

(*c*) It is thought that the contractile vacuole is formed from smaller vesicles containing fluid isotonic with the cytoplasm. Ion concentrations are then changed as a result of ion pump activity.

Explain how the data could support the hypothesis that a sodium-potassium pump may be working across the vacuole membrane but not across the plasma membrane. **3**

(5)

Marks

7. Figure 1 below shows the two alleles, *B1* and *B2*, for a gene. Within *B1* there are sites where a restriction enzyme can cut; in *B2*, the allele has a mutation at one of the restriction sites, which prevents a cut.

A probe complementary to a short portion of the DNA can bind at the position shown in Figure 1.

Figure 1

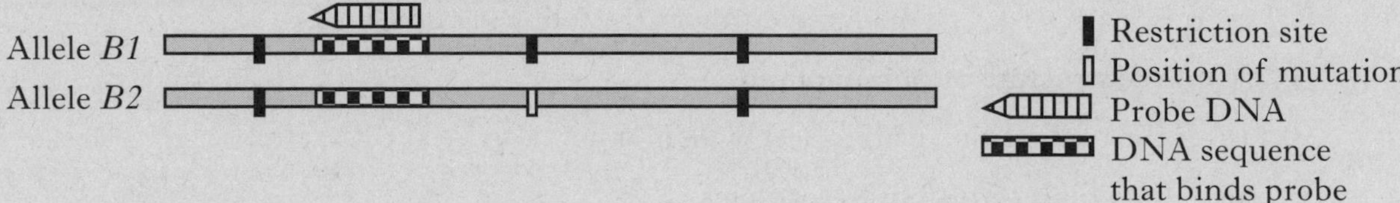

Samples of DNA from a family of two parents and their four children were digested with the same restriction enzyme. The fragments were separated by electrophoresis and tested with the probe. The results for family members are identified with the numbers 1 to 6, as shown in Figure 2.

Figure 2

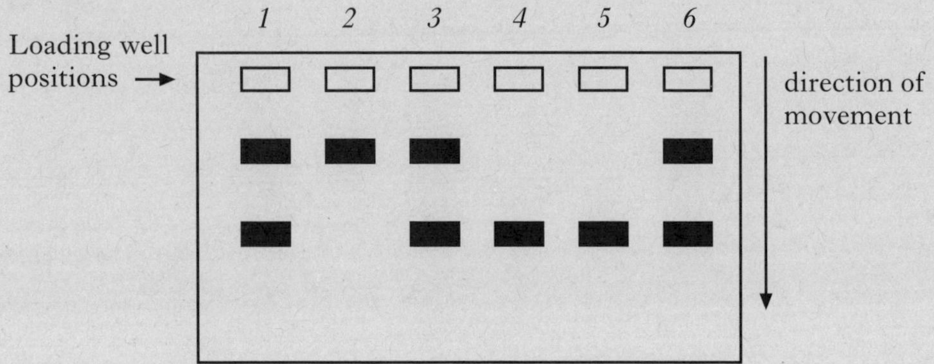

(*a*) Why is DNA able to move in the electrophoresis gel? **1**

(*b*) Explain how the results show that individuals 1, 3 and 6 have the genotype *B1B2*. **2**

(*c*) What is the genotype of individual 2? **1**

(*d*) Identify **two** individuals who could be the parents in this family. **1**

(5)

[Turn over

Marks

8. Answer **either** A **or** B.

A. Describe the growth of cells under the following headings:

(i) control mechanisms of the cell cycle; **6**

(ii) culturing of mammalian cells. **9**

(15)

OR

B. Give an account of cell membranes under the following headings:

(i) the structure of phospholipids; **6**

(ii) the composition of the plasma membrane; **3**

(iii) functions of membrane proteins. **6**

(15)

[*END OF SECTION B*]

SECTION C

Candidates should attempt questions on one unit, either Biotechnology or Animal Behaviour or Physiology, Health and Exercise.

The questions on Animal Behaviour can be found on pages 18–21.

The questions on Physiology, Health and Exercise can be found on pages 22–24.

All answers must be written clearly and legibly in ink.

Labelled diagrams may be used where appropriate.

Marks

Biotechnology

1. The diagram shows a fermenter used to grow large numbers of micro-organisms for enzyme production. To achieve rapid growth, particular conditions are needed.

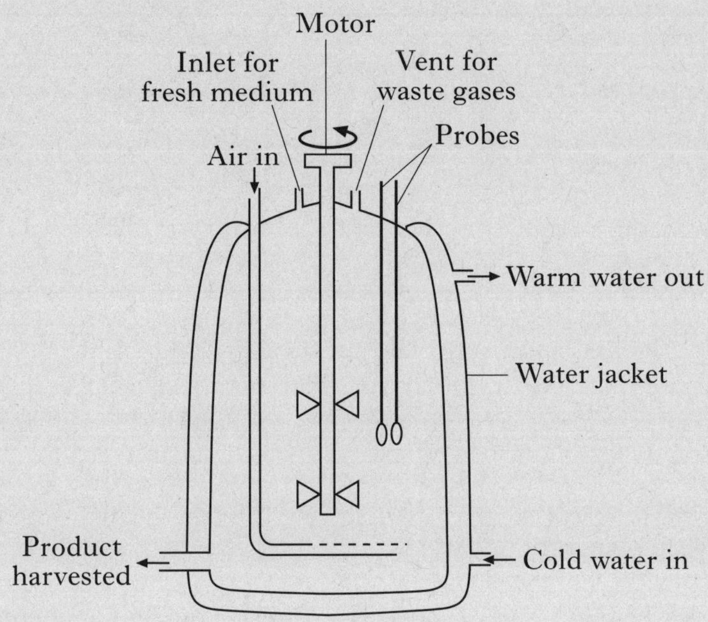

(*a*) Give **one** precaution that needs to be taken to prevent contamination by other micro-organisms during enzyme production. **1**

(*b*) Explain the purpose of the water jacket in this fermenter. **1**

(*c*) Name an enzyme produced commercially from:

(i) a naturally occurring micro-organism;

(ii) a genetically modified micro-organism. **2**

(4)

2. Antibiotics are produced commercially in large-scale industrial fermenters.

Give an account of how a pure antibiotic product could be recovered at the end of the fermentation. **(5)**

[Turn over

Biotechnology **(continued)** *Marks*

3. An investigation was carried out to determine how different energy sources affect the growth of *E. coli*. The figure shows viable counts of cells grown in three separate fermenters (A, B and C); each fermenter had a different energy source.

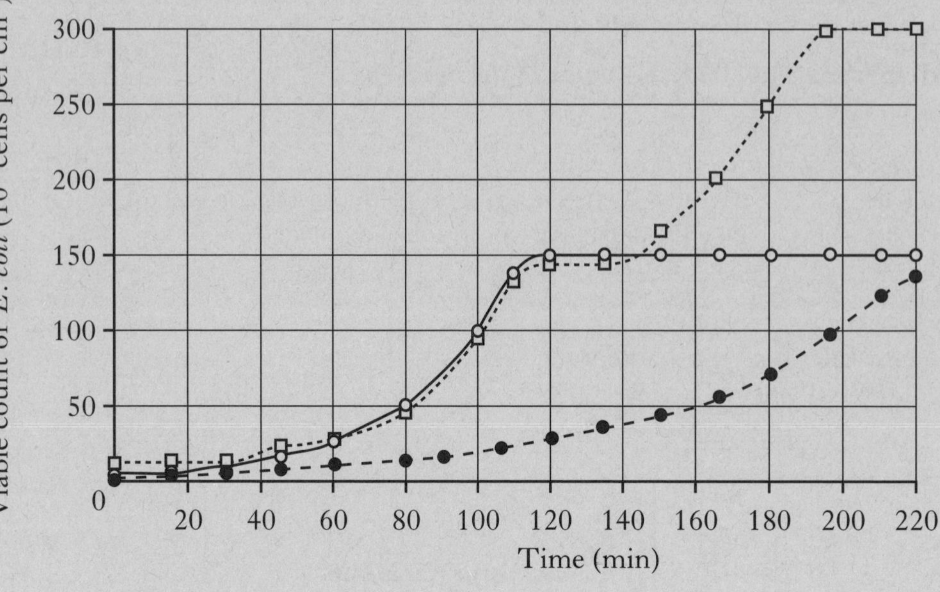

(*a*) What is the difference between a total count and a viable count? **1**

(*b*) Use data from the figure to describe how the growth of *E. coli* in 1% glucose is different from that in 1% lactose. **2**

(*c*) (i) The following equation is used to calculate the growth rate constant, k, of a bacterial population.

$k = \frac{\ln 2}{g}$, where *ln2 = 0·693* and *g* is the time in hours for the population to double.

Calculate the growth rate constant for fermenter B between 80 and 100 minutes. **1**

(ii) How could calculation of growth rate constants be used to determine when culture conditions are no longer optimal? **1**

(*d*) The diauxic growth demonstrated by *E. coli* in fermenter A is dependent on the synthesis of β-galactosidase. Briefly describe the role of CAP in stimulating the synthesis of this enzyme. **2**

(7)

Biotechnology **(continued)** *Marks*

4. Genetic manipulation of bacteria can be achieved by the introduction of plasmids containing DNA sequences from other organisms. The diagram shows a plasmid containing resistance genes for the antibiotics ampicillin and tetracycline, before and after the insertion of a DNA sequence.

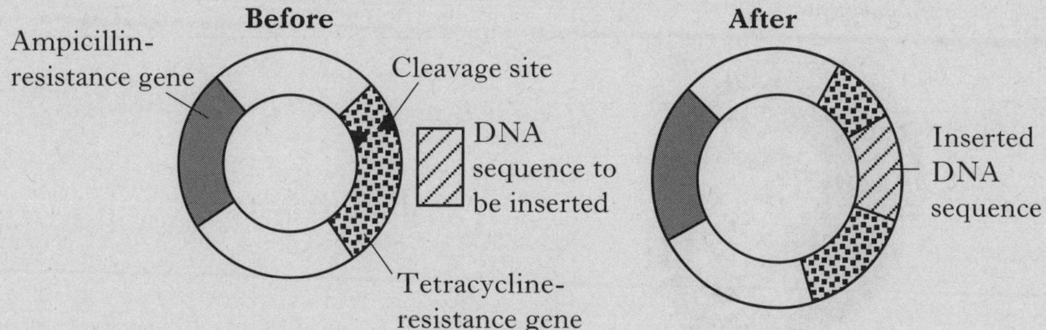

There are two possible problems with this approach:

(i) only some of the plasmids take up the DNA sequence;

(ii) only a small percentage of bacterial cells take up a plasmid of any kind.

Bacteria containing plasmids with the desirable DNA sequence can be selected by culturing them on media containing antibiotics. The same colonies are plated in the same grid positions on the two plates shown below.

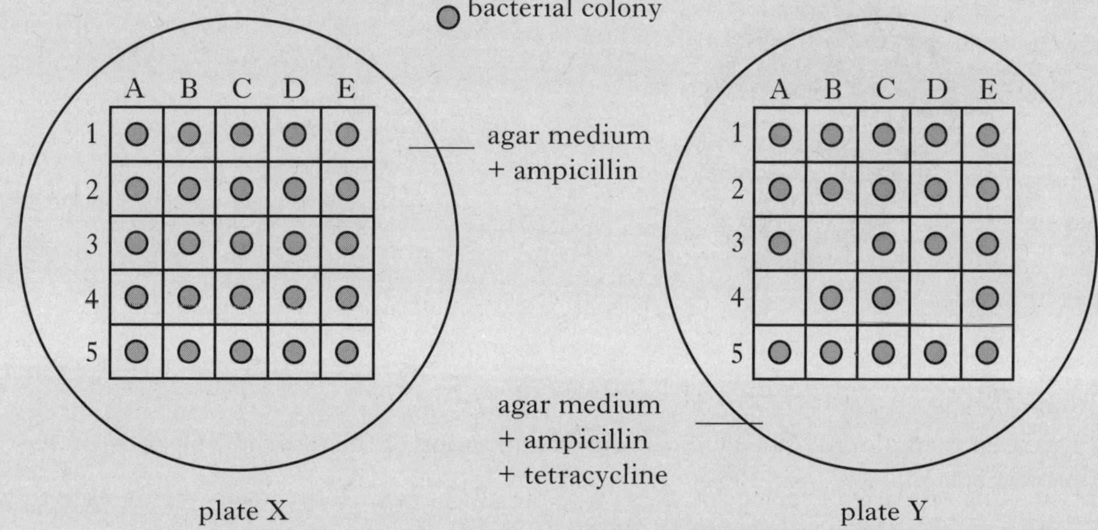

(*a*) What is the effect of inserting the DNA sequence into the tetracycline-resistance gene? **1**

(*b*) Explain why the colonies A4, B3 and D4 from plate Y would be selected for further analysis. **2**

(*c*) Give an example of an agricultural use of this technique. **1**

(4)

(20)

[End of *Biotechnology* questions. *Animal Behaviour* questions start on Page 18]

SECTION C (continued)

Marks

Animal Behaviour

1. Chimpanzees (*Pan troglodytes*) are social primates. The table shows a list of facial expressions that are used in group interactions.

Facial expression	*Interaction*
Pout 	Begging for food
Full open grin 	Displaying fear or excitement
Fear grin 	Approaching a higher-ranking chimpanzee

(*a*) What term is used to describe a list of this type? **1**

(*b*) Using an example from the table, explain the meaning of the term *anthropomorphism.* **1**

(*c*) Other than the use of facial expressions, name a behaviour in primates that is used to strengthen social bonds between the individuals in a group. **1**

(3)

Animal Behaviour **(continued)** *Marks*

2. Some males of the cichlid species *Astatotilapia burtoni* are territorial and vigorously defend their territory by fighting. Territorial males have brightly coloured bodies, a black eyebar and orange spots on their anal fin. Non-territorial males and females lack any of these bright or contrasting colours or patterns. The eggs of the females are very similar in appearance to the orange spots on the anal fins of territorial males.

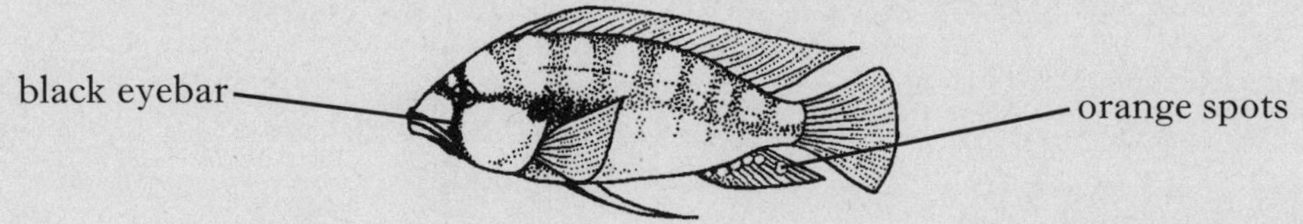

Figures 1 and 2 below show the rate of attack response of territorial males to two different dummy fish.

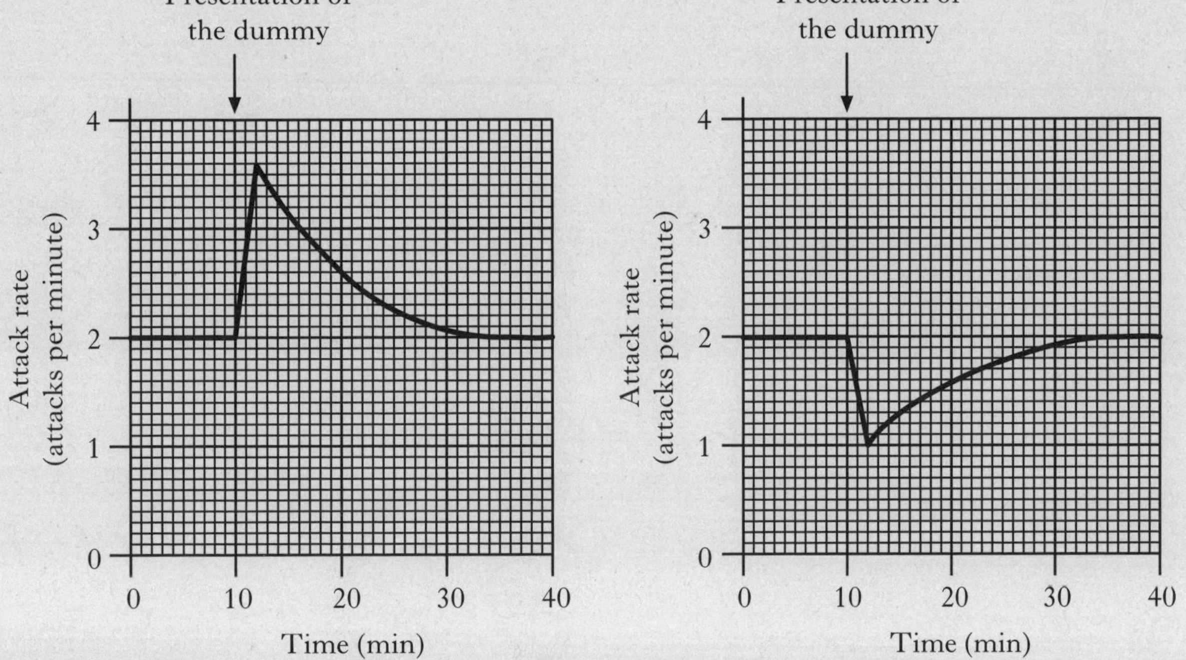

(*a*) Using data from Figures 1 and 2, compare the responses to the two dummies in relation to frequency of attacks. **2**

(*b*) Suggest an explanation for the response shown in Figure 2. **1**

(*c*) What benefit do successful males gain through fighting? **1**

(*d*) To what extent does *A. burtoni* show sexual dimorphism? **1**

[Turn over

Animal Behaviour **Question 2 (continued)** *Marks*

(*e*) The table below summarises data from experiments investigating the development of the attack response of *A. burtoni*.

Rearing conditions	*Stimuli provoking attack response*
Reared alone	Black eyebar model Male of own species
Reared by own species	Black eyebar model Male of own species
Reared by foster species	Black eyebar model Male of own species Male of foster species

What two pieces of evidence indicate that the development of attack response behaviour in *A. burtoni* depends on the interaction between genetic and environmental influences? 2

(7)

3. The cuckoo (*Cuculus canorus*) is a *brood parasite* of some species of small birds that nest in Scotland.

(*a*) What is the ultimate cause of nest-building behaviour in birds? 1

(*b*) The female cuckoo lays an egg in the host nest. Typical eggs of hosts and cuckoos are shown below.

Host species *Host species egg* *Cuckoo egg*

Species 1

Species 2

Species 3

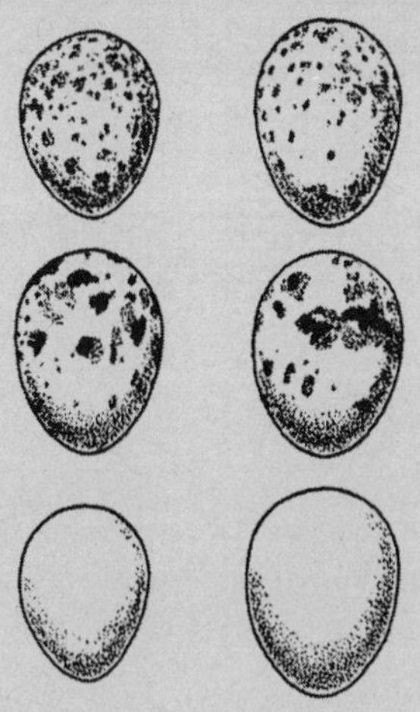

What term could be used to describe the close match in appearance between the cuckoo eggs and the host species' eggs? 1

Animal Behaviour **Question 3 (continued)** *Marks*

(*c*) The figure shows the feeding behaviour of a young cuckoo.

The hatchling cuckoo bears little resemblance to the host's hatchlings.

What compels the host to feed the young cuckoo? **1**

(*d*) Explain why the relationship between the host and the cuckoo is **not** an example of reciprocal altruism. **2**

(5)

4. Imprinting is a feature of bird behaviour.

Discuss the process of imprinting. **(5)**

(20)

[End of *Animal Behaviour* questions. *Physiology, Health and Exercise* questions start on Page 22]

[Turn over

SECTION C (continued)

Marks

Physiology, Health and Exercise

1. Two patients were tested for diabetes in hospital. After fasting, their blood glucose was measured at 09:00 hours. They were given a glucose drink and their blood glucose was monitored over the following 3 hours (Glucose Tolerance Test). The test results are shown below.

City General Hospital

OUTPATIENTS DEPARTMENT

Name *Patient A*

Glucose Tolerance Test

Time	Blood Glucose Concentration (mmol/L)
09:00	*4·4*
09:30	*6·8*
10:00	*6·1*
10:30	*5·4*
11:00	*5·3*
11:30	*4·9*
12:00	*4·5*

City General Hospital

OUTPATIENTS DEPARTMENT

Name *Patient B*

Glucose Tolerance Test

Time	Blood Glucose Concentration (mmol/L)
09:00	*7·8*
09:30	*11·7*
10:00	*13·9*
10:30	*15·0*
11:00	*16·1*
11:30	*15·5*
12:00	*15·5*

(*a*) Give **two** pieces of evidence from the test results that could be used to identify the diabetic patient. **2**

(*b*) What is the role of glucagon in the control of blood glucose concentration? **1**

(*c*) (i) State the major risk factor in the onset of non insulin-dependent diabetes mellitus (NIDDM). **1**

(ii) Give **two** ways by which regular exercise can help in the control of NIDDM. **2**

(6)

Physiology, Health and Exercise **(continued)** *Marks*

2. Basal metabolic rate (BMR) can be calculated using the following equations:

Males
Age 10–17 years: BMR(MJ/day) = 0·074 × body mass (kg) + 2·754
Age 18–29 years: BMR(MJ/day) = 0·063 × body mass (kg) + 2·896

Females
Age 10–17 years: BMR(MJ/day) = 0·056 × body mass (kg) + 2·898
Age 18–29 years: BMR(MJ/day) = 0·062 × body mass (kg) + 2·036

(*a*) Calculate the basal metabolic rate for a 26 year old woman with a mass of 75 kg. **1**

(*b*) Energy expenditure can be determined by measuring the oxygen uptake from breathed air. Explain why this procedure is referred to as indirect calorimetry. **1**

(*c*) Explain how different factors affect BMR. **5**

(7)

3. The table shows data from maximal testing of an individual, before and after a period of endurance training. The data can be used to calculate $VO_{2\,max}$.

Measurement	*Before training*	*After training*
Left ventricular mass (g)	210	300
Maximum stroke volume (ml)	120	180
Maximum heart rate (beats/min)	175	195
Maximum oxygen uptake (L/min)	3·1	4·6
Body mass (kg)	60	60

(*a*) Which measurements from the table would be used to calculate:

(i) $VO_{2\,max}$ **1**

(ii) cardiac output? **1**

(*b*) What evidence from the table indicates that this individual has developed cardiac hypertrophy? **1**

(*c*) Describe how $VO_{2\,max}$ is determined using sub-maximal testing. **1**

(4)

[Turn over for Question 4 on *Page twenty four*

Physiology, Health and Exercise **(continued)** *Marks*

4. The force exerted by the blood against the walls of blood vessels is known as blood pressure. The figure shows changes in arterial blood pressure of a 20 year old female and a 45 year old male.

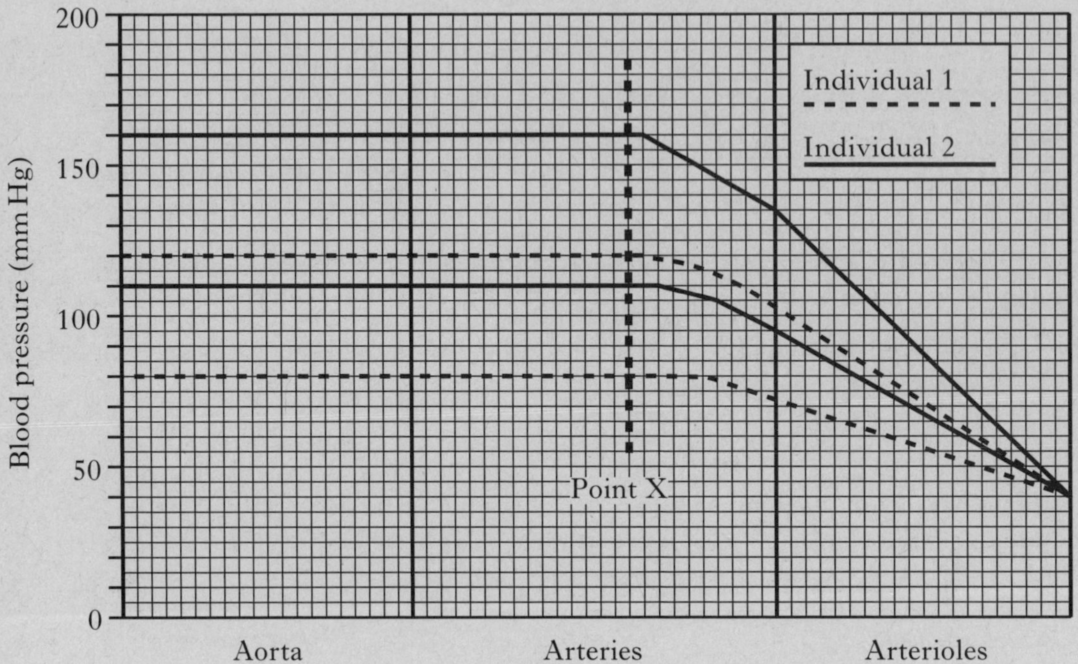

A medical examination showed that the 45 year old had hypertension.

(*a*) State **two** modifiable conditions that can influence the development of hypertension. **2**

(*b*) What is the diastolic blood pressure of the 45 year old man at point X on the graph? **1**

(3)

(20)

[*END OF QUESTION PAPER*]

ADVANCED HIGHER

2008

[BLANK PAGE]

X007/701

NATIONAL QUALIFICATIONS 2008

TUESDAY, 27 MAY
1.00 PM – 3.30 PM

BIOLOGY
ADVANCED HIGHER

SECTION A—Questions 1–25 (25 marks)

Instructions for completion of Section A are given on *Page two*.

SECTIONS B AND C

The answer to each question should be written in ink in the answer book provided. Any additional paper (if used) should be placed inside the front cover of the answer book.

Rough work should be scored through.

Section B (55 marks)

All questions should be attempted. Candidates should note that Question 8 contains a choice.

Question 1 is on Pages 10, 11 and 12. Questions 2, 3 and 4 are on Page 13. Pages 12 and 13 are fold-out pages.

Section C (20 marks)

Candidates should attempt the questions in **one** unit, **either** Biotechnology **or** Animal Behaviour **or** Physiology, Health and Exercise.

Read carefully

1 Check that the answer sheet provided is for **Biology Advanced Higher (Section A)**.

2 For this section of the examination you must use an **HB pencil** and, where necessary, an eraser.

3 Check that the answer sheet you have been given has **your name**, **date of birth**, **SCN** (Scottish Candidate Number) and **Centre Name** printed on it.

Do not change any of these details.

4 If any of this information is wrong, tell the Invigilator immediately.

5 If this information is correct, **print** your name and seat number in the boxes provided.

6 The answer to each question is **either** A, B, C or D. Decide what your answer is, then, using your pencil, put a horizontal line in the space provided (see sample question below).

7 There is **only one correct** answer to each question.

8 Any rough working should be done on the question paper or the rough working sheet, **not** on your answer sheet.

9 At the end of the exam, put the **answer sheet for Section A inside the front cover of the answer book**.

Sample Question

Which of the following molecules contains six carbon atoms?

A Glucose

B Pyruvic acid

C Ribulose bisphosphate

D Acetyl coenzyme A

The correct answer is **A**—Glucose. The answer **A** has been clearly marked in **pencil** with a horizontal line (see below).

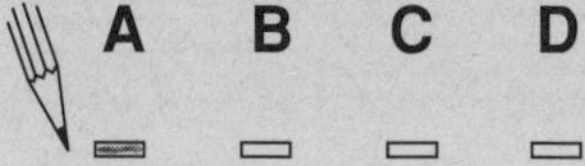

Changing an answer

If you decide to change your answer, carefully erase your first answer and using your pencil, fill in the answer you want. The answer below has been changed to **D**.

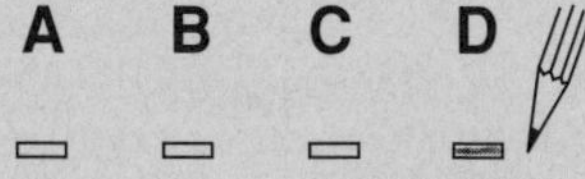

SECTION A

All questions in this section should be attempted.

Answers should be given on the separate answer sheet provided.

1. Which of the following genes encode proteins that promote normal cell division?

A Oncogenes

B Regulatory genes

C Proliferation genes

D Anti-proliferation genes

2. The cell cycle is believed to be monitored at checkpoints where specific conditions must be met for the cycle to continue.

Condition 1: chromosome alignment

Condition 2: successful DNA replication

Condition 3: cell size

Which line in the table correctly shows the condition fulfilled at each checkpoint?

	G1	*G2*	*M*
A	2	3	1
B	3	1	2
C	2	1	3
D	3	2	1

3. Which line in the table correctly describes the chemical reaction that breaks down a disaccharide into its monomer subunits?

	Type of reaction	*Type of bond broken*
A	hydrolysis	peptide
B	condensation	glycosidic
C	hydrolysis	glycosidic
D	condensation	peptide

4. An unbranched polysaccharide is made up of glucose monomers joined together by $\beta(1\rightarrow4)$ linkages. The polysaccharide described could be

A amylose

B amylopectin

C glycogen

D cellulose.

5. Which of the following is a covalent bond that stabilises the tertiary structure of a protein?

A Hydrogen bond

B Disulphide bond

C Glycosidic bond

D Ester linkage

6. In the diagrams below, the sugar-phosphate backbone of a DNA strand is represented by a vertical line showing 5' to 3' polarity. The horizontal lines between bases represent hydrogen bonds.

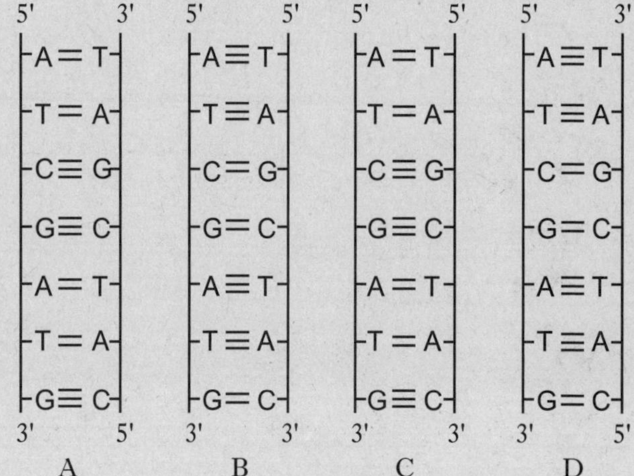

Which diagram represents correctly a short stretch of a DNA molecule?

7. If ten percent of the bases in a molecule of DNA are adenine, what is the ratio of adenine to guanine in the same molecule?

A 1:1

B 1:2

C 1:3

D 1:4

[Turn over

8. Which line in the table below correctly summarises the movement of sodium and potassium ions into and out of a cell by a sodium-potassium pump?

	Potassium ions	*Sodium ions*
A	in	out
B	in	in
C	out	in
D	out	out

9. Which of the following is a component of the cytoskeleton?

A Phospholipid
B Tubulin
C Peptidoglycan
D Glycoprotein

10. A length of DNA is cut into fragments by the restriction enzymes BamHI and EcoRI

▼ BamHI cut site
△ EcoRI cut site

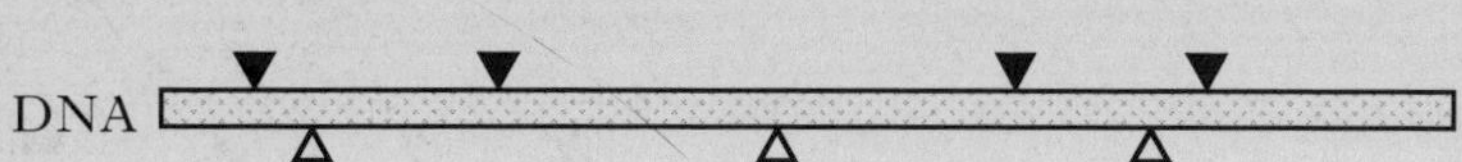

Which line in the table below correctly identifies the number of DNA fragments obtained?

	DNA cut by BamH1 only	*DNA cut by EcoR1 only*	*DNA cut by both BamH1 and EcoR1*
A	5	4	8
B	4	5	8
C	5	4	9
D	4	5	9

11. The diagram below outlines the stages involved in the polymerase chain reaction.

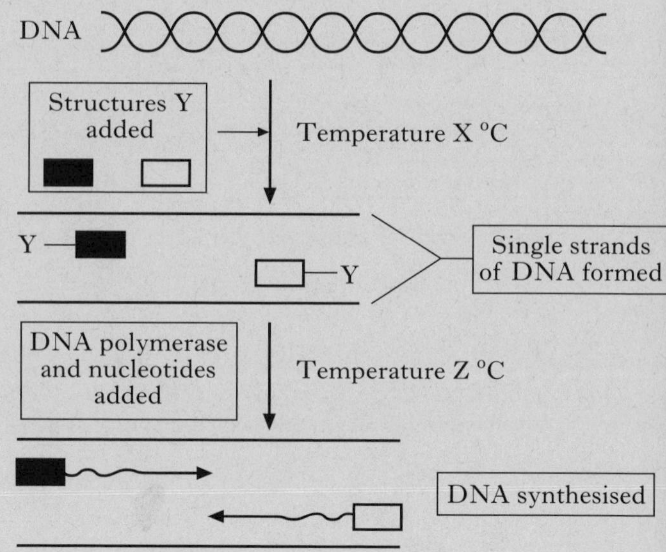

Which line in the table correctly identifies temperature X and the structures labelled Y?

	Temperature X (°C)	*Structure Y*
A	55	probe
B	95	primer
C	55	primer
D	95	probe

12. The result of profiling various DNA samples in a criminal investigation is shown below.

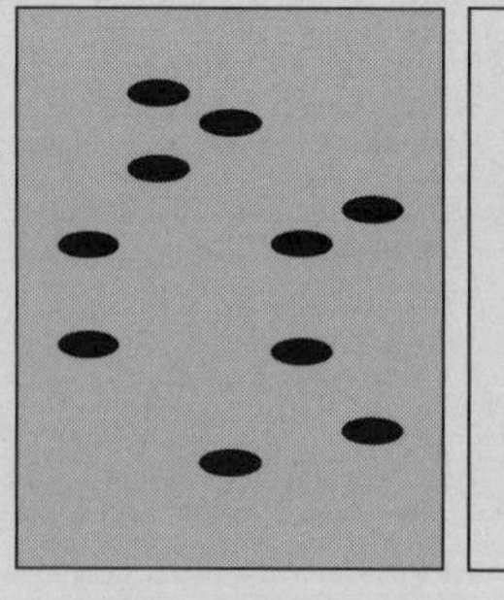

Key:
1 blood sample of victim
2 blood sample of suspect X
3 blood sample of suspect Y
4 first sample from forensic evidence
5 second sample from forensic evidence

Which of the following could the DNA analyst conclude about the crime?

A Only suspect X was involved
B Only suspect Y was involved
C Suspects X and Y were both involved
D Neither suspect X nor Y was involved

13. Which of the following micro-organisms is responsible for the conversion of nitrite to nitrate in soil?

A *Nitrobacter*

B *Pseudomonas*

C *Nitrosomonas*

D *Rhizobium*

Questions 14 and 15 relate to the diagram below, which shows the recycling of carbon in the environment.

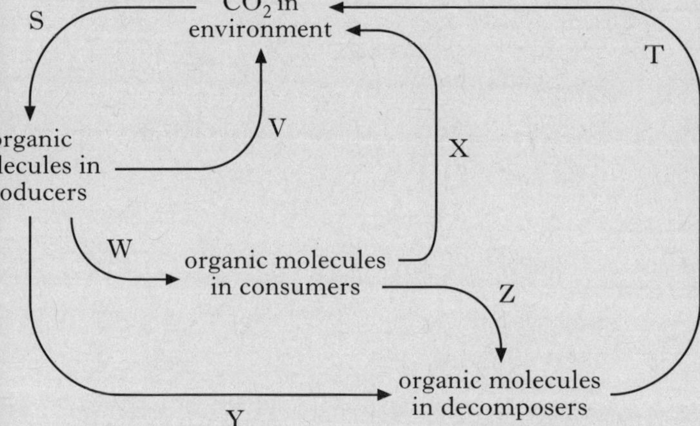

14. Which line in the table below describes correctly the processes that are occurring at stages S, V and W?

	Transformation	*Fixation*	*Respiration*
A	W	S	V
B	W	V	S
C	V	S	W
D	S	W	V

15. Coral bleaching could increase if process S is

A greater than V + X + T

B greater than W + Y + Z

C less than W + Y + Z

D less than V + X + T.

16. Which line in the table matches a group of organisms correctly with their type of nutrition?

	Group of organisms	*Type of nutrition*
A	producers	heterotrophic
B	consumers	autotrophic
C	decomposers	autotrophic
D	consumers	heterotrophic

17. Population size can be estimated using the following formula:

$$P = \frac{n_1 \times n_2}{n_3}$$

where P = population estimate

n_1 = number first captured, marked and released

n_2 = total number in second capture

n_3 = number of marked individuals recaptured.

In a survey to estimate a woodlouse population, the following data were obtained:

Woodlice captured, marked and released = 40
Marked woodlice in second capture = 12
Unmarked woodlice in second capture = 48

The estimated population of the woodlice was

A 100

B 160

C 200

D 1920.

18. Which of the following is a density-independent effect?

A A decrease in temperature increasing the abundance of a tree species.

B An increase in food supply increasing the abundance of a herbivore.

C A decrease in predators increasing the abundance of a prey species.

D An increase in competitors decreasing the yield of a crop species.

[Turn over

19. The figure shows the results of red deer population surveys in two areas of the same size.

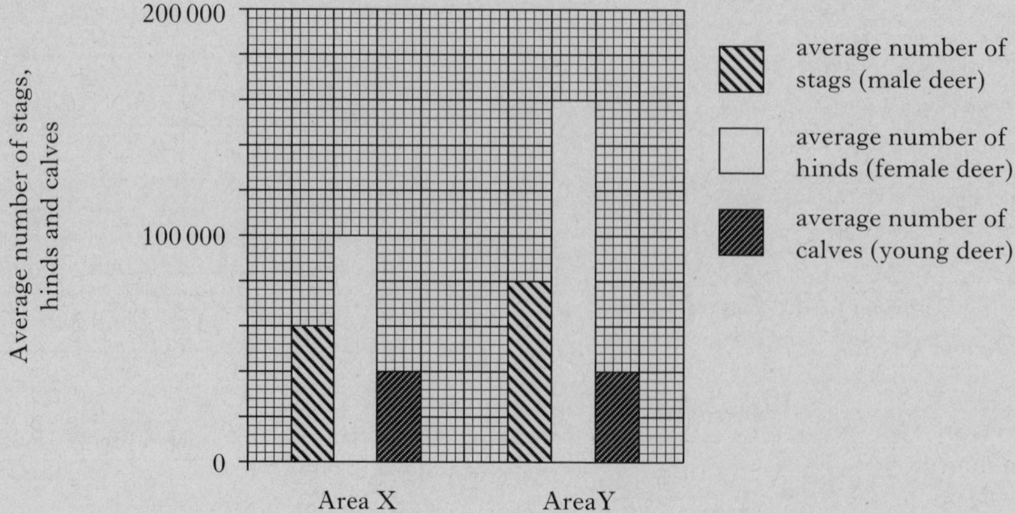

Which line in the table below correctly shows the effect of a change in population density on the birth rate of red deer?

	Population density	*Proportion of hinds having calves*
A	increases	decreases
B	decreases	decreases
C	increases	increases
D	decreases	stays the same

20. Parasitism is a form of symbiosis. A parasite that is facultative

A benefits from its host but does not harm it

B can be associated with a host but can also live independently

C is passed to its main host from a secondary host

D has a relationship with its host from which both benefit.

21. The marine iguana (*Amblyrhyncus cristatus*) of the Galapagos Islands basks in the sunshine before swimming for food in the cold sea water. Which line of the table correctly describes the iguana and its temperature regulating mechanism?

	Type of organism	*Mechanism*
A	homeothermic	behavioural
B	homeothermic	physiological
C	poikilothermic	behavioural
D	poikilothermic	physiological

22. The Puerto Rican lizard *Anolis cristatellus* is found both in shaded forests and in open sunlit areas.

The graph below shows the relationship between air temperature and body temperature of lizards occupying each habitat.

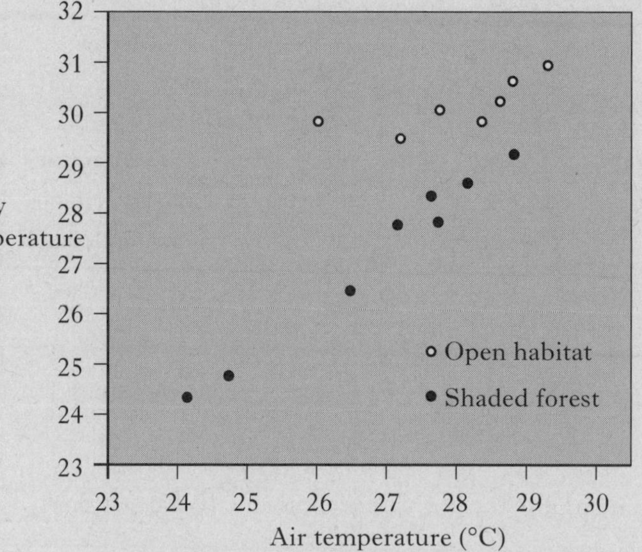

Which line in the table shows the response of the lizards to changes in air temperature in each habitat?

	Open habitat	*Shaded forest habitat*
A	regulation	regulation
B	regulation	conformation
C	conformation	conformation
D	conformation	regulation

23. Common terns (*Sterna hirundo*) feed on fish and nest colonially on land. Nesting terns often attempt to steal fish from neighbouring terns in their colony.

What term describes correctly this type of competitive interaction?

A Exploitation competition

B Interference competition

C Competitive exclusion

D Resource partitioning

24. The diagram below shows the distribution of two species of barnacle. The fundamental and realised niches of the two species are shown by the vertical lines W, X, Y and Z. The realised niche of species 2 is line Z.

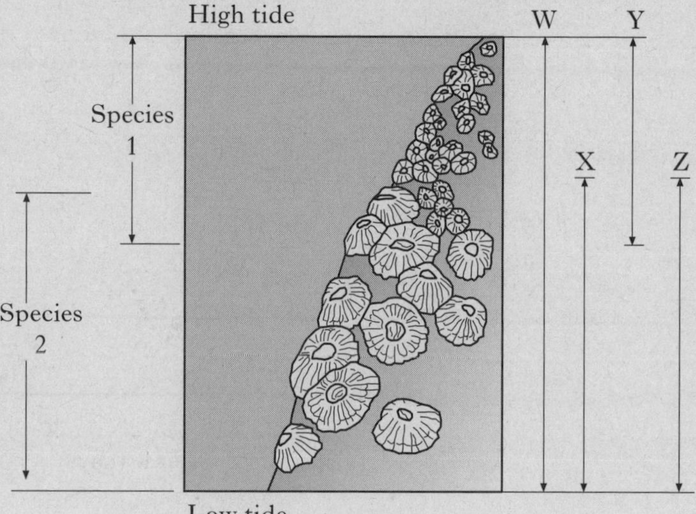

Which line in the table below identifies correctly the other niches?

	Fundamental niche of species 1	*Fundamental niche of species 2*	*Realised niche of species 1*
A	W	X	Y
B	Y	X	W
C	W	Y	X
D	X	W	Y

[Turn over

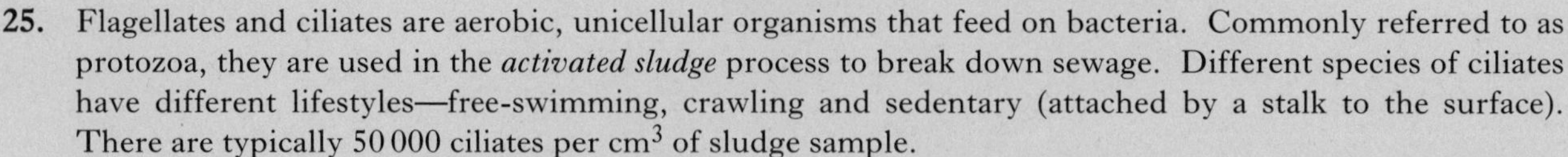

25. Flagellates and ciliates are aerobic, unicellular organisms that feed on bacteria. Commonly referred to as protozoa, they are used in the *activated sludge* process to break down sewage. Different species of ciliates have different lifestyles—free-swimming, crawling and sedentary (attached by a stalk to the surface). There are typically 50 000 ciliates per cm^3 of sludge sample.

The graph shows succession in the development of activated sludge.

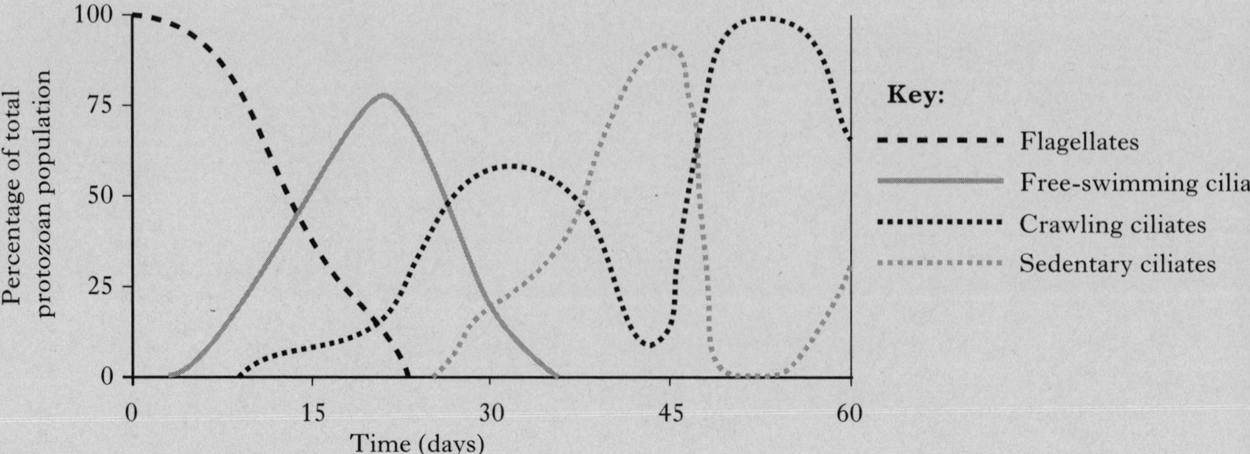

On which day in the succession would a sample contain 30 000 per cm^3 crawling and 10 000 per cm^3 free-swimming ciliates?

A 15

B 20

C 30

D 35

[END OF SECTION A]

Candidates are reminded that the answer sheet MUST be returned INSIDE the front cover of the answer book.

[Turn over for Section B on *Page ten*

SECTION B

All questions in this section should be attempted.
All answers must be written clearly and legibly in ink.

1. In 1992, a membrane protein called *aquaporin-1* (AQP1) was found to function exclusively as a channel for the passage of water molecules. The AQP1 molecule spans the phospholipid bilayer; each of its four linked subunits is a separate water channel (Figure 1).

Figure 1: Aquaporin-1 in a membrane

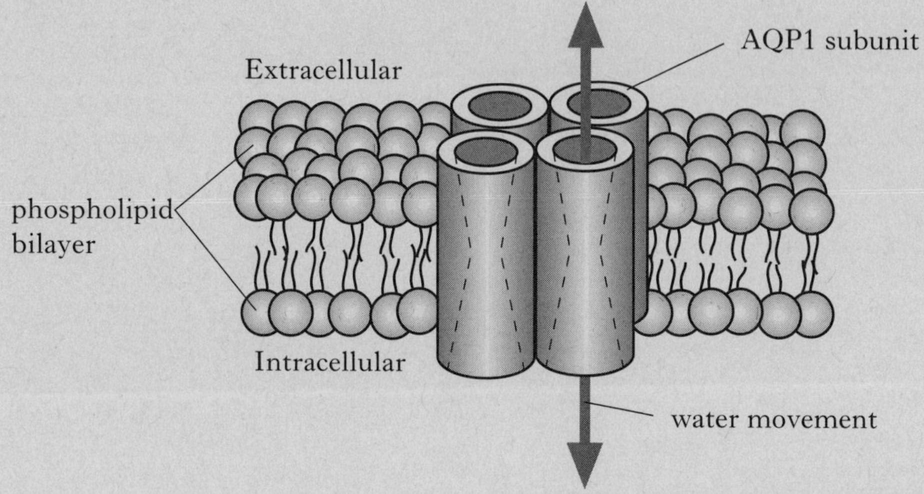

Early experiments were designed to determine the role of these protein channels in water movement. Researchers removed the contents of red blood cells to leave structures consisting of only the plasma membranes; these are known as "red cell ghosts". The ghosts were filled with solutions containing radioactive water and the concentration gradient across the membrane was varied. The rate at which water molecules moved out of the ghosts was measured in isotonic and hypertonic external solutions, before and after a treatment that inactivates AQP1.

From their results, summarised in the Table, the researchers concluded that the very rapid transfer of water across membranes during osmosis was through the AQP1 channels.

Table: Rate of water movement across ghost membranes

	Rate of water movement (units s^{-1})	
External solution	*Untreated AQP1*	*Treated AQP1*
Isotonic	2·5	1·0
Hypertonic	20	1·8

Recent studies have shown that several different aquaporins exist and they are present in a number of organs including eyes, brain, lungs and kidneys; all of them are important in water transport across membranes. In kidneys, they are found in some parts of the nephrons (Figure 2) where they have a role in water balance.

Question 1 (continued)

Figure 2: Nephron

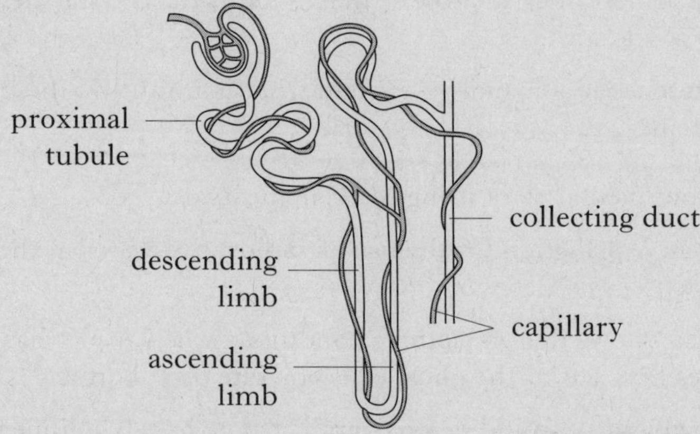

AQP1 is present only in the cells lining the proximal tubule, descending limb and in the capillaries associated with the nephron. About 70% of the water entering the nephron is reabsorbed here. A different aquaporin, AQP2, is present in cells of the collecting duct. The number of AQP2 molecules active at a cell surface increases with the concentration of antidiuretic hormone (ADH) in blood. ADH secretion is increased so that more water is reabsorbed into the capillaries from urine in the duct.

To study the importance of aquaporins in kidney function, three groups of mice with different genotypes were selected.

Group 1: genotype NN: homozygous for the presence of AQP1;

Group 2: genotype Nn: heterozygous;

Group 3: genotype nn: homozygous recessive; AQP1 absent.

Body mass and urine solute concentration were measured before and after a period without water. The results are shown in Figure 3 and Figure 4.

Figure 3: % change in body mass of mice after a period without water

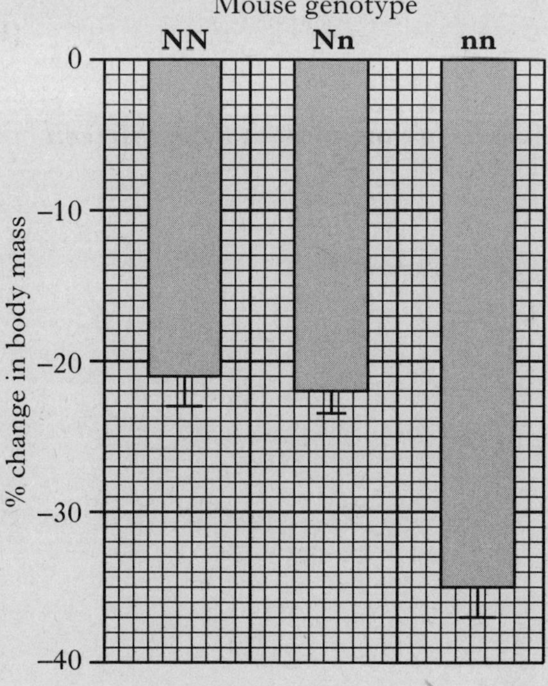

Figure 4: Urine solute concentration before (H) and after (D) a period without water

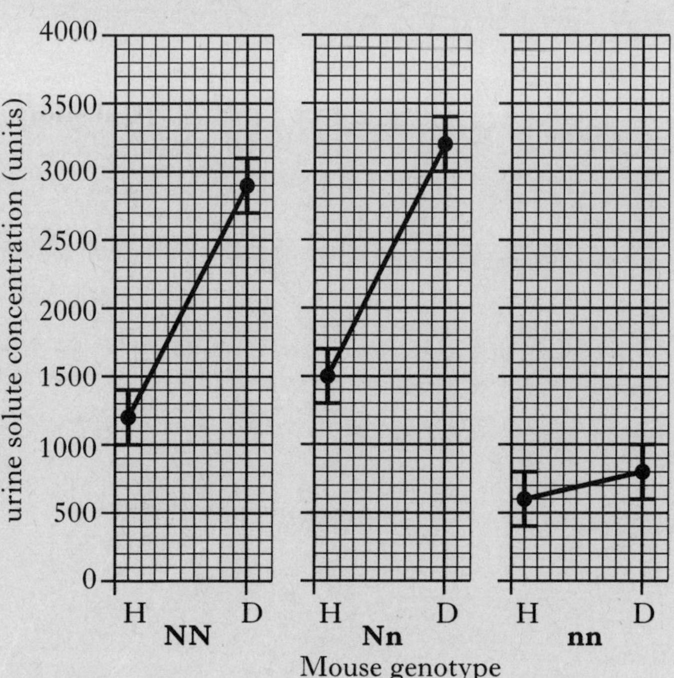

[Question 1 continues on *Page twelve*

Marks

Question 1 (continued)

(*a*) (i) What term describes a protein that is embedded in a membrane rather than attached to the surface? **1**

(ii) With reference to aquaporin, explain what is meant by the quaternary structure of a protein. **1**

(*b*) Refer to the experimental work using red cell ghosts.

(i) Suggest an explanation for the use of radioactive water in the solutions placed in the ghosts. **1**

(ii) The Table shows that in isotonic conditions when AQP1 has been treated, water molecules flow out of the ghost cells at a rate of 1·0 units s^{-1}.

Explain why there would be no overall change in cell volume in these conditions. **1**

(iii) Aquaporins were inactivated by phosphorylation.

Which type of enzyme adds phosphate to a protein? **1**

(iv) Use data from the Table to show that functioning aquaporins can increase water flow across a membrane by over 1000%. **2**

(*c*) (i) Figure 3 shows that homozygous recessive mice lost about 35% of their body mass during the period when they had no water supply.

Explain how these results may lead to the conclusion that the homozygous recessive mice lost abnormally high amounts of water in their urine. **2**

(ii) Refer to Figure 3 and Figure 4. Use the data to show that heterozygous mice are producing enough AQP1 molecules for normal osmoregulation. **3**

(*d*) Humans with a condition called *nephrogenic diabetes insipidus* (NDI) have normal AQP1 and ADH production but have non-functioning AQP2.

(i) Predict the effect of a period of dehydration on urine production by individuals with NDI compared to individuals without NDI. **1**

(ii) Explain your prediction. **1**

(14)

[Questions 2, 3 and 4 are on fold-out *Page thirteen*

Marks

2. (*a*) (i) Identify structure X shown in the diagram below. 1

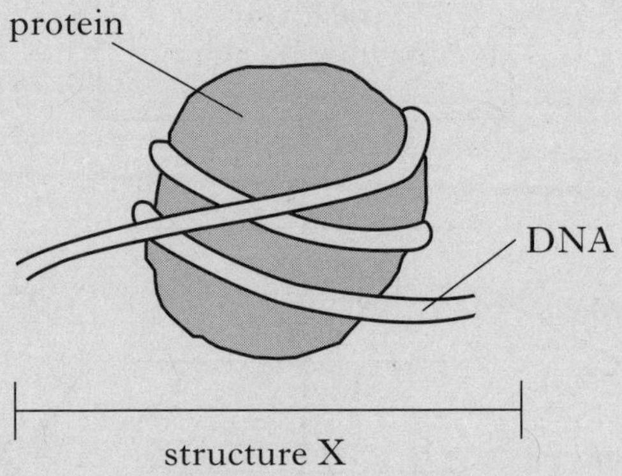

(ii) Why is the binding of DNA to this type of protein so important for eukaryotic cells? 2

(*b*) In the production of transgenic plants, the genome of a plant species can be modified by incubating protoplasts with engineered plasmids.

(i) Name the prokaryotic species used as the source of these plasmids. 1

(ii) Describe how protoplasts are produced from isolated plant cells. 1

(5)

3. Describe the general structure of steroids and their function in cell signalling. **(4)**

4. The diagram below represents an enzyme, PRPP synthetase, involved at the start of the biochemical pathway that produces nucleotides. In the active site there are two positions (S) where the substrate molecules, ribose and ATP, bind and react. Position I is an inhibitor binding site and position A is an activator binding site.

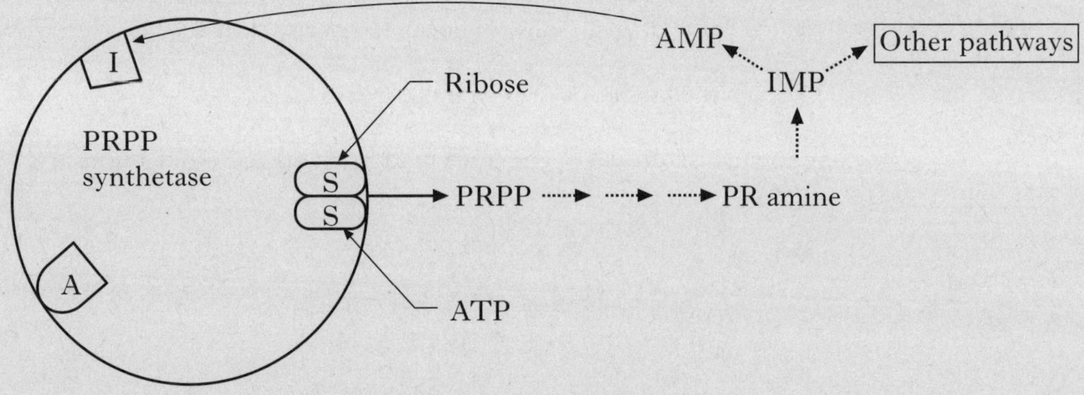

(*a*) What is meant by induced fit when referring to enzyme action? 1

(*b*) Explain why PRPP synthetase is described as an allosteric enzyme. 1

(*c*) Describe the effect of AMP formation on the metabolic pathway. 2

(4)

Marks

5. The diagram below shows energy flow through a deciduous forest ecosystem. Units are kJ m^{-2} day^{-1}.

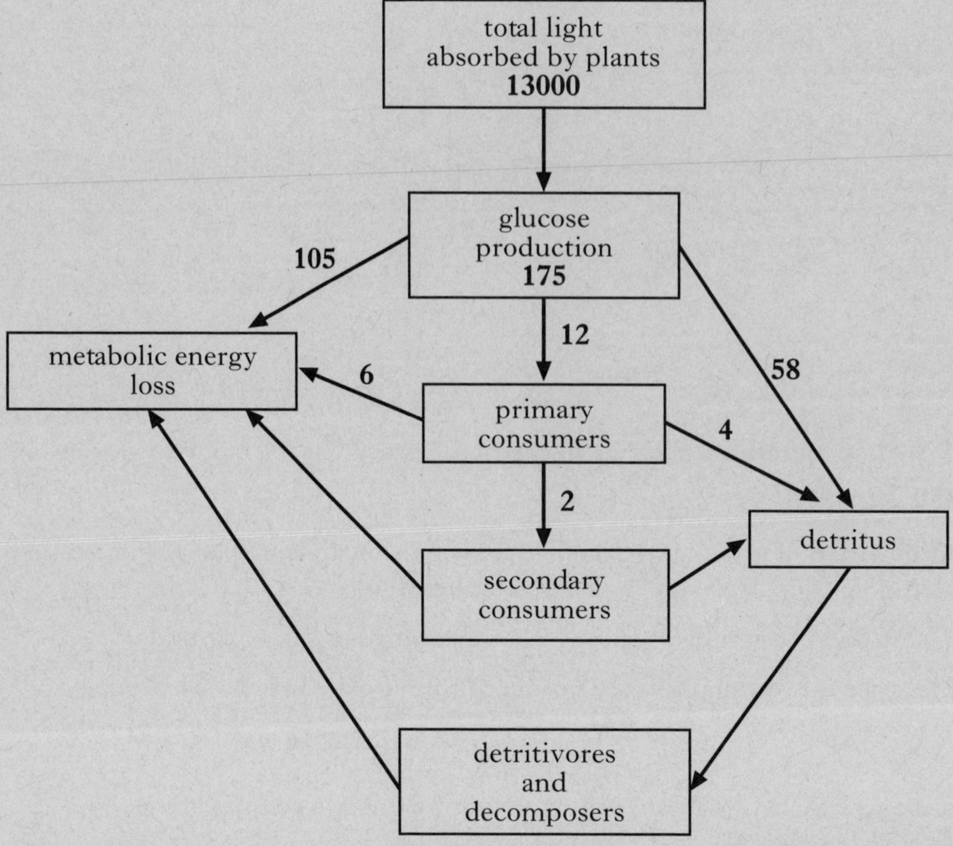

(*a*) Calculate the percentage of light energy that is captured in photosynthesis by the forest plants. **1**

(*b*) What is the value for net primary productivity (NPP) in this ecosystem? **1**

(*c*) Ten percent is often quoted as a typical value for ecological efficiency. Use the data to show that this value does not always apply to energy transfer between trophic levels. **1**

(*d*) In what form is the energy lost from metabolism? **1**

(*e*) Compare the use of digestive enzymes by detritivores and decomposers. **1**

(5)

Marks

6. The figure below shows processes in the nitrogen cycle that rely on the activities of micro-organisms.

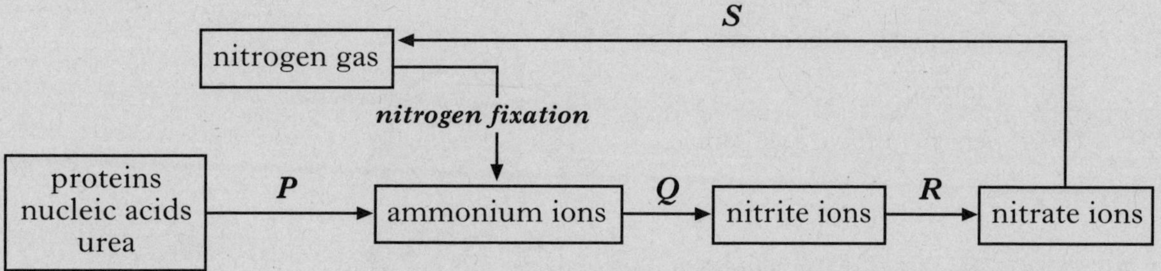

(*a*) The bacteria responsible for processes Q and R are *obligate aerobes*.

What does this term suggest about their metabolic requirements? **1**

(*b*) Nitrogen fixation is often the product of a prokaryote–eukaryote symbiosis. It depends on the action of an enzyme system that functions best in anaerobic conditions.

(i) Identify a prokaryote involved in such an interaction. **1**

(ii) Name the enzyme responsible for nitrogen fixation. **1**

(iii) What is the role of leghaemoglobin in this interaction? **1**

(*c*) State the likely effect of process S on soil fertility in aerobic conditions. **1**

(5)

7. Rust fungi are pathogens of many monocultures. In infected plants, *pustules* are formed that are responsible for the spread of infection.

The figure below shows the spread of a rust fungus from a single infected plant.

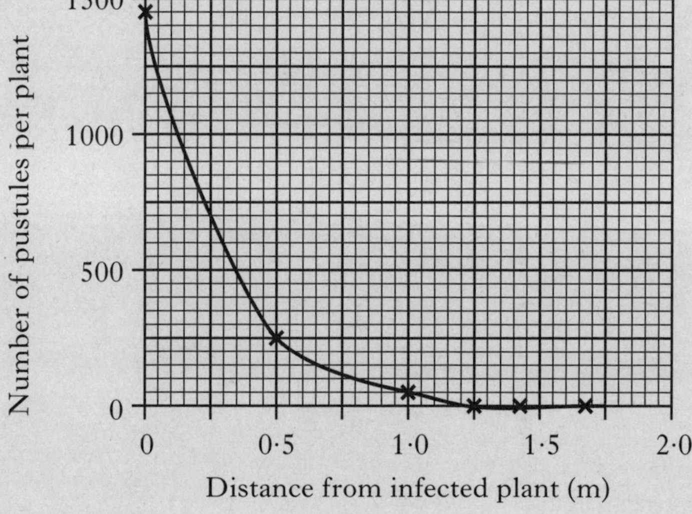

(*a*) Define the term monoculture. **1**

(*b*) What do the data suggest about the spacing needed to prevent the fungus infection from spreading? **1**

(*c*) Apart from altering spacing, suggest another way of growing rust-free crops. **1**

(3)

Marks

8. Answer **either** A **or** B.

A. Discuss how ecosystems may be affected by the following:

(i) phosphate enrichment; **5**

(ii) exotic species; **4**

(iii) persistent toxic pollutants. **6**

(15)

OR

B. Discuss the roles of the following in the survival of organisms:

(i) dormancy; **7**

(ii) mimicry; **4**

(iii) mutualism. **4**

(15)

[*END OF SECTION B*]

SECTION C

Candidates should attempt questions on one unit, either Biotechnology or Animal Behaviour or Physiology, Health and Exercise.

The questions on Animal Behaviour can be found on pages 20–22.

The questions on Physiology, Health and Exercise can be found on pages 23–25.

All answers must be written clearly and legibly in ink.

Labelled diagrams may be used where appropriate.

Marks

Biotechnology

1. (*a*) The Figure below shows the growth curve of a bacterium.

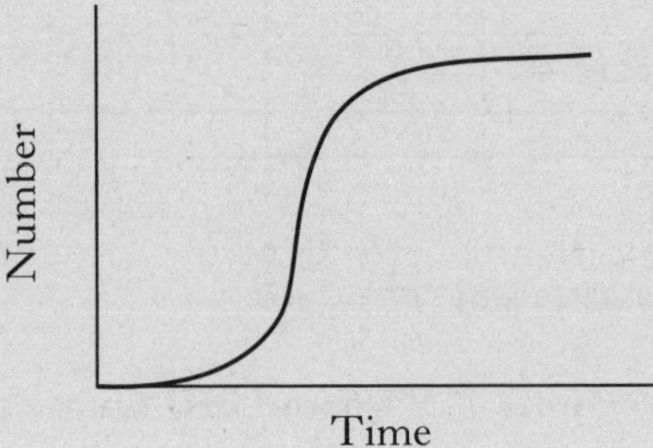

Give **two** reasons why there is only a small change in the number of bacteria during the lag phase. **2**

(*b*) A haemocytometer is used to estimate cell numbers. The diagram below shows part of a haemocytometer grid. The depth of the chamber is 0·1 mm.

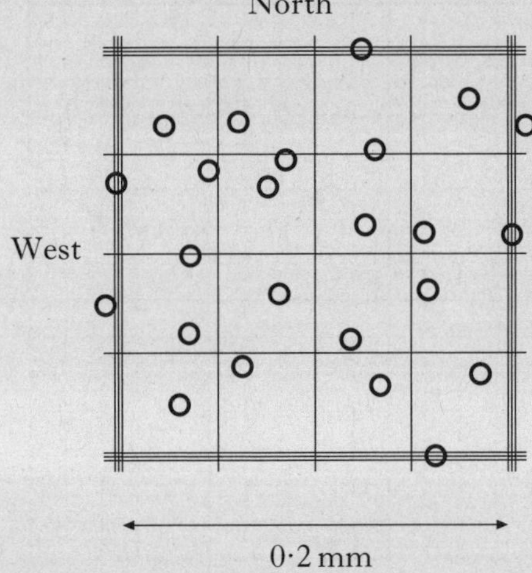

(i) One precaution taken when using the grid is to exclude cells overlapping the north and west sides.

What is the purpose of this precaution? **1**

(ii) Calculate the number of cells in 1 mm^3 of the sample shown on the haemocytometer grid. **1**

(*c*) (i) Penicillin is an antibiotic that is described as *bacteriostatic*.

Distinguish between *bacteriostatic* activity and *bactericidal* activity. **1**

(ii) Name an antibiotic other than penicillin. **1**

(*d*) Antibodies are produced in response to the presence of foreign antigens.

(i) Name the cells that secrete antibodies. **1**

(ii) Give **one** medical use of monoclonal antibodies. **1**

(8)

Biotechnology **(continued)** *Marks*

2. Explain how genetic modification of the "*flavrsavr*" tomato plant has resulted in fruit with longer shelf life. **(4)**

3. (*a*) The nitrogen content of two yeast extracts, BW6 and BK1, is shown in the Table below.

	Yeast extract	
	BW6	*BK1*
Total nitrogen (g/100 g)	7·1	11·9
% of nitrogen as amino acids	34	56

The figure below shows the effect on the growth of the bacterium *Lactobacillus casei* of adding different proportions of BW6 and BK1.

Figure: Effect of varying proportions of BW6 and BK1 on the growth of *L. casei*

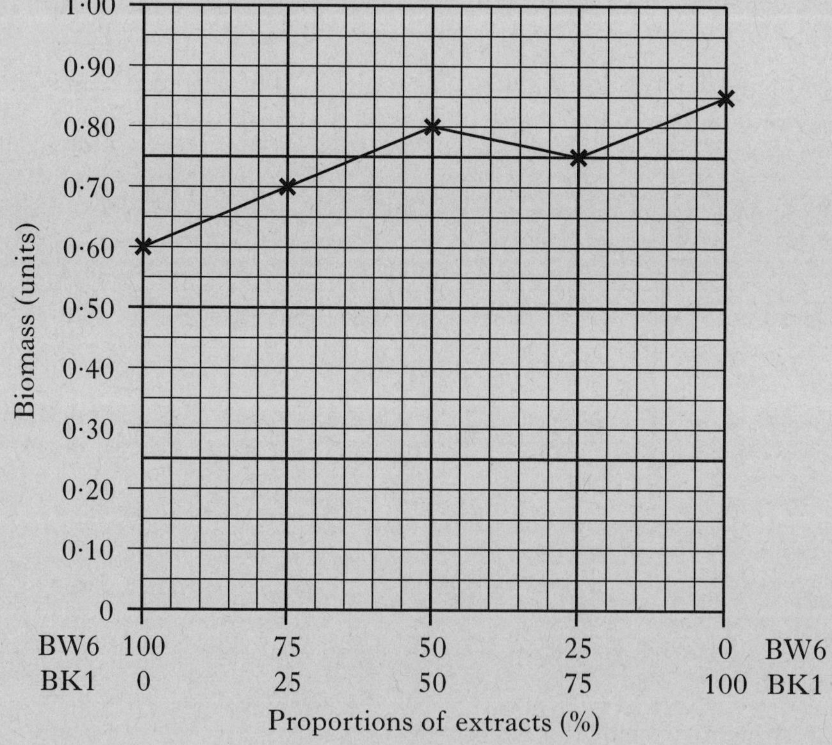

(i) Use the data to describe the effect of varying the proportions of the extracts on the growth of the bacterium. 2

(ii) Suggest a reason for this effect on *L. casei*. 1

(*b*) Give one agricultural use of *Lactobacillus* species. 1

(4)

Biotechnology **(continued)** *Marks*

4. Different yeast species are cultured to create large quantities of yeast cell biomass. Some of the biomass is destined for activities such as brewing and baking while much of the biomass is treated to bring about autolysis. The *autolysate* produced has a variety of uses, for example as a nutrient source in fermentation media.

(*a*) What is meant by the term *autolysis*? **1**

(*b*) State **two** factors that could influence the characteristics of yeast autolysate. **2**

(*c*) Yeast extract is prepared from the autolysate.

State one use of yeast extract in the food industry. **1**

(4)

(20)

[End of *Biotechnology* questions. *Animal Behaviour* questions start on Page 20]

[Turn over

SECTION C (continued)

Marks

Animal Behaviour

1. The woodlouse *Hemilepistus reaumuri* lives in deserts. To avoid drying out, it digs a burrow from which it ventures each day to forage.

Figure: Life cycle of *H. reaumuri*

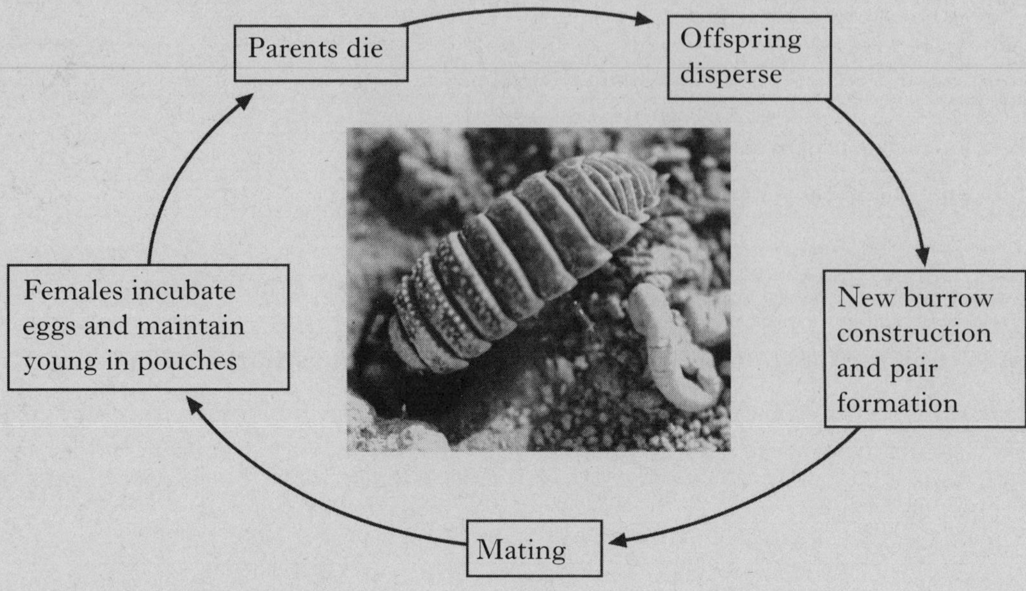

(*a*) After dispersal, both males and females can begin new burrows, or they can attempt to pair with an existing burrower.

Why are larger males more successful than smaller ones in pair formation with a female that has already started a burrow? **1**

(*b*) Suggest proximate and ultimate causes for burrow digging in this species. **2**

(*c*) For *H. reaumuri*, state one reason why the parental investment of females is higher than that of males. **1**

(*d*) After foraging, these woodlice show an *innate* ability to navigate straight back to their burrows.

What is meant by the term innate? **1**

(*e*) State the effect of an increased encounter rate and a reduced handling time on the duration of foraging. **1**

(6)

Animal Behaviour **(continued)** *Marks*

2. The fire ant *Solenopsis invicta* is a social insect found in South America. A study of kin selection showed that colonies of *S. invicta* can have either of two distinct social structures, *compact* colonies or *sprawling* colonies.

Compact colonies contain ants that are all produced by a single female, the queen. The workers in compact colonies are loyal to the queen and are aggressive towards intruders. In contrast, large sprawling colonies, which are becoming more common, are formed from many interconnected nests inhabited by many queens.

The difference in social structure depends on the presence or absence of allele B of the gene *GP-9*. Ants with the B allele produce a receptor protein that enables them to distinguish the odours of ants from different genetic backgrounds.

(*a*) What is meant by the term *kin selection*? **1**

(*b*) Allele B is only found in compact colonies.

Explain how the absence of allele B has led to the formation of the sprawling colony. **2**

(*c*) Give another example of a single gene effect. **1**

(4)

3. Discuss the role of dispersal in the avoidance of inbreeding in birds and mammals.

Why is it important for animals to avoid inbreeding and how is this achieved? **(4)**

[Turn over

Animal Behaviour **(continued)** *Marks*

4. The success of herring gull (*Larus argentatus*) foraging behaviour was studied using video recordings. Herring gulls have adult plumage after 4 years; the age of younger birds can be determined by other visible characteristics.

The Figure shows the mean feeding rates for herring gulls in different age classes.

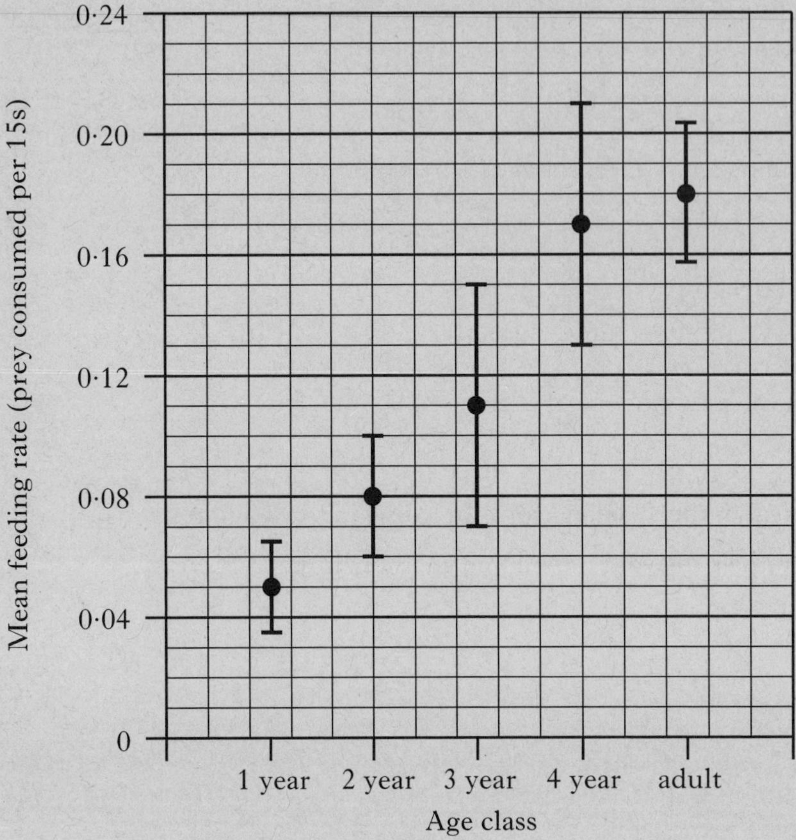

(*a*) (i) Identify **two** age classes between which there is a significant difference in foraging success. **1**

(ii) Suggest an explanation for the trend seen in the feeding rate. **1**

(iii) An adult feeding at 0·18 prey per 15 seconds takes 83 seconds to capture one prey item.

How long would it take a one-year-old to capture one prey item? **1**

(*b*) Suggest **one** advantage of using video recording for this analysis. **1**

(*c*) Describe **two** ways in which herring gulls have successfully adapted to human influence. **2**

(6)

(20)

[End of *Animal Behaviour* questions. *Physiology, Health and Exercise* questions start on Page 23]

SECTION C (continued)

Marks

Physiology, Health and Exercise

1. A stent is a narrow, wire mesh tube that can be inserted into a blood vessel. It may be used to treat atherosclerosis in the blood vessels of the heart. Figure 1 shows a blood vessel before and after the procedure to insert a stent.

Figure 1

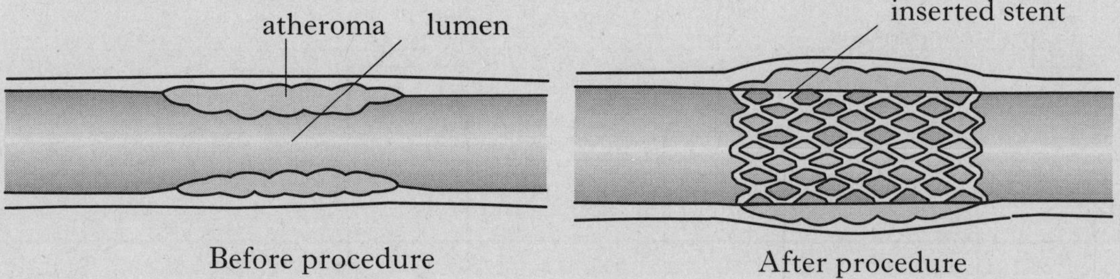

(*a*) Name the blood vessels that deliver blood to the myocardium. **1**

(*b*) Describe how *atherosclerosis* develops. **2**

(*c*) Figure 2 shows the volume changes in a blood vessel in the heart as a result of a stent being fitted.

Figure 2

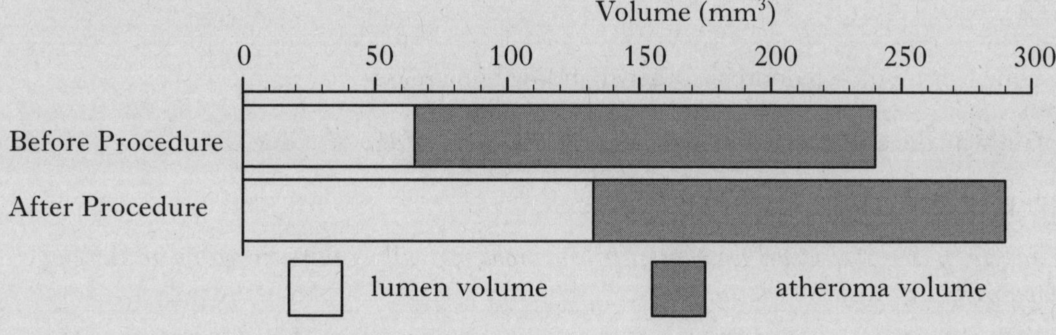

(i) Use the data to explain how the procedure achieves increased blood flow. **2**

(ii) What term is used for the chest pain relieved by this procedure? **1**

(6)

[Turn over

Physiology, Health and Exercise **(continued)** *Marks*

2. The data show trends expected in the numbers of American women who have low bone mass and who will go on to develop osteoporosis.

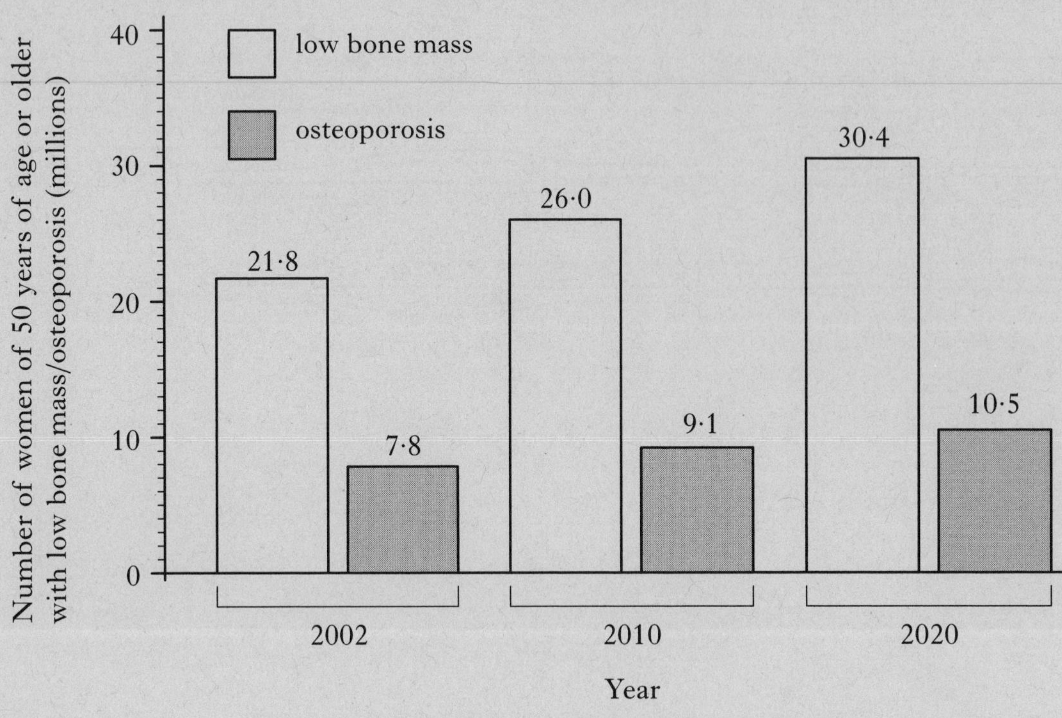

(*a*) Give one feature of osteoporosis other than low bone mass. **1**

(*b*) Explain why the study focuses on women of 50 years of age or older. **1**

(*c*) Authors of the research claimed that:

"*In future, fewer American women with hip problems will eventually go on to develop osteoporosis.*"

(i) Suggest how critics could use the data provided to contradict this claim. **1**

(ii) How did the authors use the data to arrive at their conclusion? **1**

(*d*) Explain why American teenagers would be advised to take up jogging rather than swimming to reduce the risk of osteoporosis. **2**

(6)

Physiology, Health and Exercise **(continued)** *Marks*

3. (*a*) The table shows data relating to four members of a group trying to achieve different weight-loss targets. The energy deficit value indicates the severity of their intended diet. Dietary weight loss is assumed to be from fat loss.

A negative energy balance of 29·4 MJ is required to lose 1 kg.

Group member	*Present weight* (kg)	*Target weight* (kg)	*Energy deficit* (MJ/day)
A	96	91	2
B	121	113	3
C	104	98	2
D	92	82	3

(i) How many days will individual **D** take to reach the target weight? **1**

(ii) Individual **A** is 1·74m in height. Calculate this individual's body mass index (BMI). **1**

(*b*) Explain why being "overweight" does not always mean that someone is unhealthy. **1**

(*c*) Name a method of measuring body composition. **1**

(4)

4. Discuss the use of exercise testing in the assessment of aerobic fitness. **(4)**

(20)

[*END OF QUESTION PAPER*]

[BLANK PAGE]

ADVANCED HIGHER

2009

[BLANK PAGE]

X007/701

NATIONAL QUALIFICATIONS 2009

THURSDAY, 28 MAY
1.00 PM – 3.30 PM

BIOLOGY
ADVANCED HIGHER

SECTION A—Questions 1–25 (25 marks)

Instructions for completion of Section A are given on *Page two*.

SECTIONS B AND C

The answer to each question should be written in ink in the answer book provided. Any additional paper (if used) should be placed inside the front cover of the answer book.

Rough work should be scored through.

Section B (55 marks)

All questions should be attempted. Candidates should note that Question 8 contains a choice.

Question 1 is on Pages 10, 11 and 12. Questions 2, 3 and 4 are on Page 13. Pages 12 and 13 are fold-out pages.

Section C (20 marks)

Candidates should attempt the questions in **one** unit, **either** Biotechnology **or** Animal Behaviour **or** Physiology, Health and Exercise.

LI X007/701 6/7520

Read carefully

1 Check that the answer sheet provided is for **Biology Advanced Higher (Section A)**.

2 For this section of the examination you must use an **HB pencil** and, where necessary, an eraser.

3 Check that the answer sheet you have been given has **your name**, **date of birth**, **SCN** (Scottish Candidate Number) and **Centre Name** printed on it.

Do not change any of these details.

4 If any of this information is wrong, tell the Invigilator immediately.

5 If this information is correct, **print** your name and seat number in the boxes provided.

6 The answer to each question is **either** A, B, C or D. Decide what your answer is, then, using your pencil, put a horizontal line in the space provided (see sample question below).

7 There is **only one correct** answer to each question.

8 Any rough working should be done on the question paper or the rough working sheet, **not** on your answer sheet.

9 At the end of the exam, put the **answer sheet for Section A inside the front cover of the answer book**.

Sample Question

Which of the following molecules contains six carbon atoms?

A Glucose

B Pyruvic acid

C Ribulose bisphosphate

D Acetyl coenzyme A

The correct answer is **A**—Glucose. The answer **A** has been clearly marked in **pencil** with a horizontal line (see below).

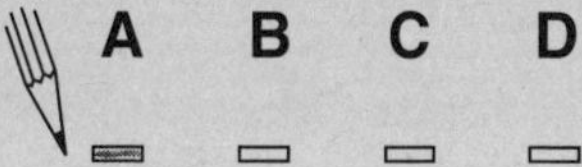

Changing an answer

If you decide to change your answer, carefully erase your first answer and using your pencil, fill in the answer you want. The answer below has been changed to **D**.

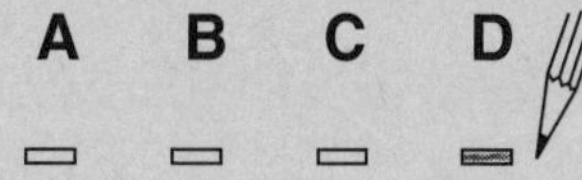

SECTION A

All questions in this section should be attempted.

Answers should be given on the separate answer sheet provided.

1. The diagram shows a bacterial cell.

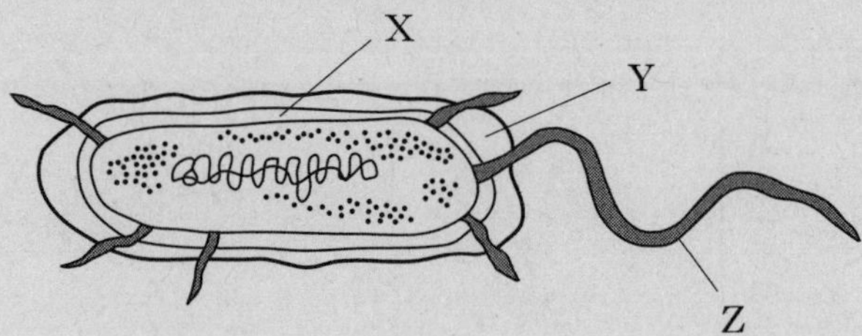

Which line in the table below correctly identifies the labelled structures?

	X	*Y*	*Z*
A	cell wall	capsule	flagellum
B	capsule	cell wall	flagellum
C	cell wall	capsule	pilus
D	capsule	cell wall	pilus

2. Which of the following diagrams best represents the sequence of phases involved in the cell cycle?

A

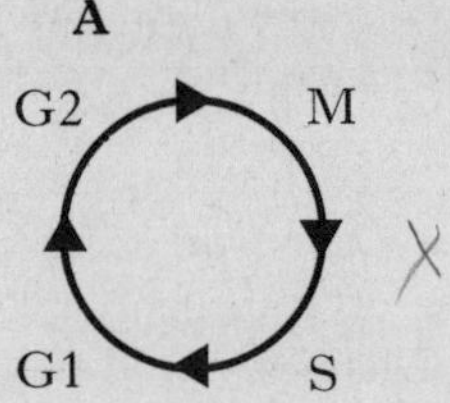

B

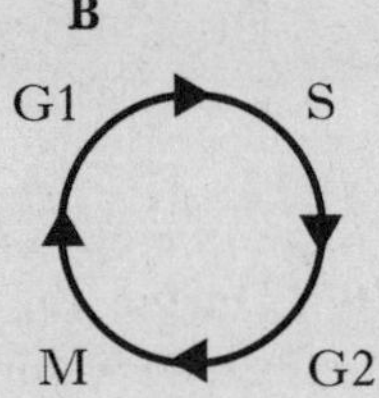

C

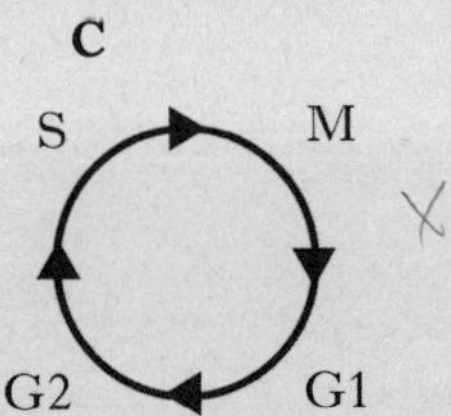

D

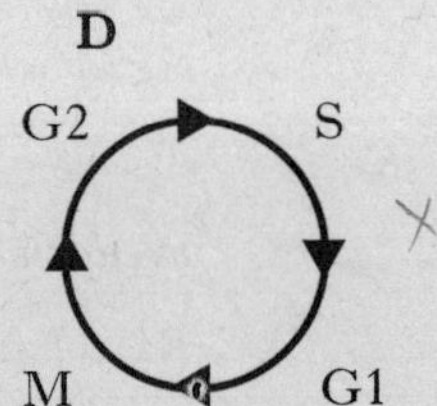

3. The covalent chemical bonds between nucleotides in DNA are

A peptide

B phosphodiester

C glycosidic

D hydrogen.

4. Which line in the table below classifies correctly the four bases in DNA as either purines or pyrimidines?

	Purines	*Pyrimidines*
A	adenine and thymine	cytosine and guanine
B	cytosine and guanine	adenine and thymine
C	cytosine and thymine	adenine and guanine
D	adenine and guanine	cytosine and thymine

5. The table below shows the number of cells from a cell culture at different points in the cell cycle.

Stage	*Number of cells*
Interphase	462
Prophase	23
Metaphase	24
Anaphase	4
Telophase	16

The mitotic index of the sample is

A 14·5%

B 12·7%

C 85·5%

D 74·7%.

[Turn over

6. The percentage of adenine bases in a double stranded DNA molecule is 30% and in a single stranded RNA molecule it is 25%.

Which line in the table below shows the number of other bases in each molecule for which the percentage could be calculated?

	RNA	*DNA*
A	none	three
B	none	none
C	one	two
D	one	three

7. During a biochemical reaction the transfer of a phosphate group from one molecule to another is catalysed by

A ligase

B ATPase

C kinase

D nuclease.

8. The diagram below shows an enzyme-catalysed reaction.

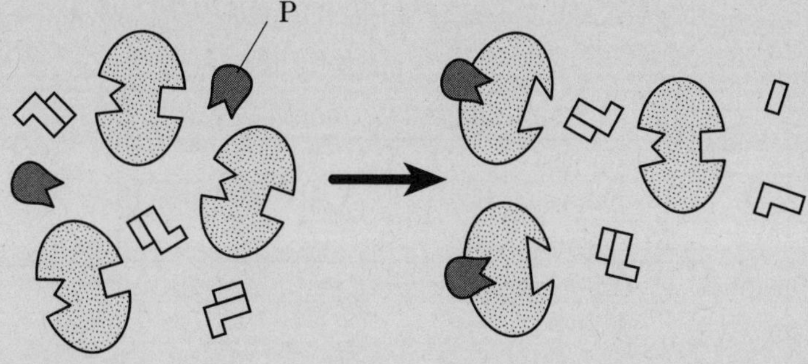

Which of the following correctly identifies molecule P?

A Substrate

B Activator

C Competitive inhibitor

D Non-competitive inhibitor

9. The diagram below shows the changes in the activity of enzymes that synthesise tryptophan and utilise lactose in a cell after the addition of tryptophan and lactose.

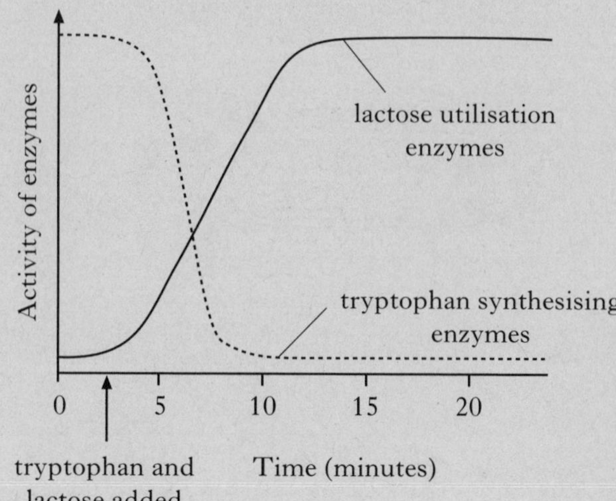

What valid conclusion may be made from the graph?

A Addition of lactose acts as a negative enzyme modulator.

B Addition of tryptophan acts as a positive enzyme modulator.

C Enzyme induction is occurring in lactose utilisation enzymes.

D Enzyme induction is occurring in tryptophan synthesising enzymes.

10. During the production of transgenic plants, which of the following bacteria would be used to transfer recombinant plasmids into plant protoplasts?

A *Agrobacterium*

B *E. coli*

C *Pseudomonas*

D *Rhizobium*

11. The diagram below shows the restriction enzyme sites in a plasmid that carries the genes for resistance to the antibiotics ampicillin and tetracycline.

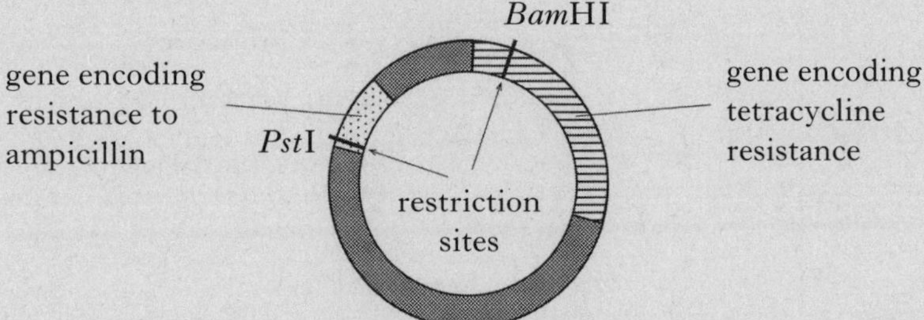

Which line in the table below identifies correctly the antibiotic resistance that would remain when a gene is inserted at these restriction enzyme sites?

	Gene inserted into restriction enzyme site	*Antibiotic resistance remaining*
A	*Bam*HI	tetracycline and ampicillin
B	*Pst*I	ampicillin
C	*Pst*I	tetracycline and ampicillin
D	*Bam*HI	ampicillin

12. A piece of DNA was digested using the restriction enzymes *Bam*HI and *Eco*RI. The results are shown below.

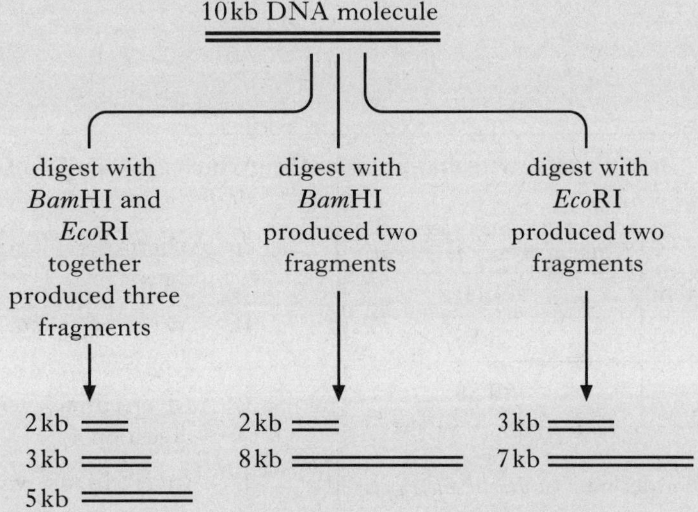

Which of the following restriction maps can be drawn from these results?

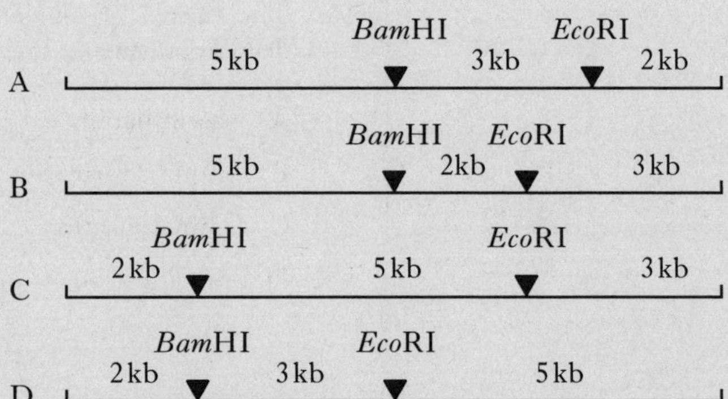

13. The graph below shows variation in biomass throughout one year in an aquatic ecosystem.

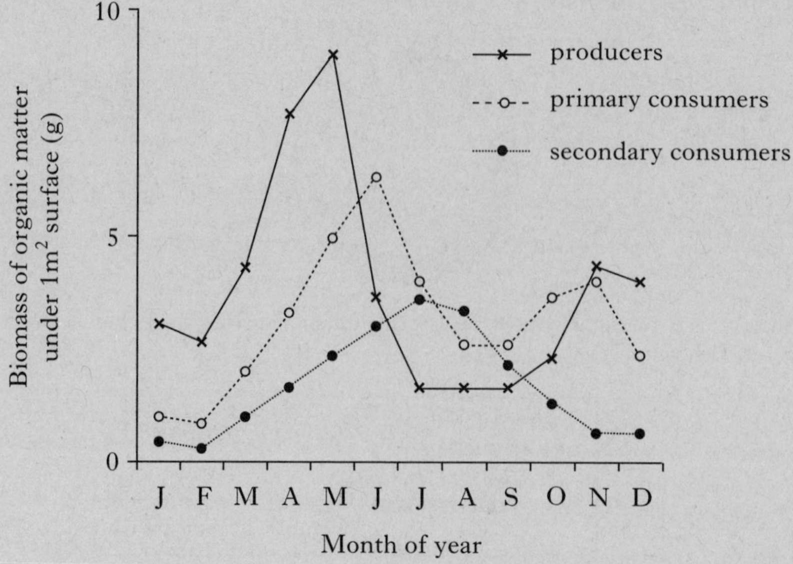

During which month of the year would the following pyramid of biomass be applicable?

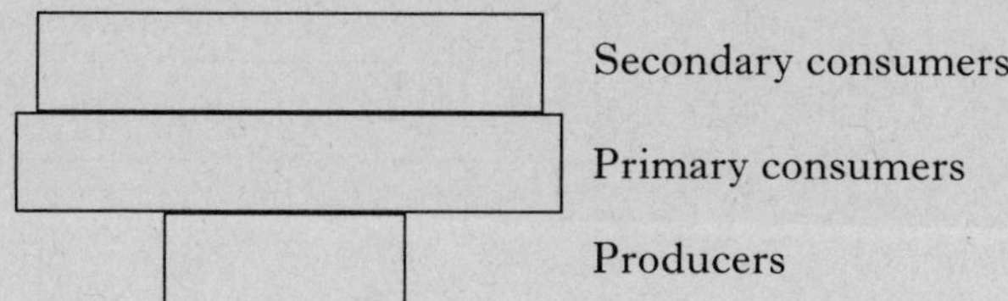

A June

B July

C August

D September

14. The table below shows measurements of energy in a grassland ecosystem.

	Units of energy m^{-2} $year^{-1}$
Solar energy entering ecosystem	471·00
Fixed in photosynthesis	5·83
Released in respiration by autotrophs	0·88

What is the net productivity (*units of energy m^{-2} $year^{-1}$*) for this ecosystem?

A 4·95

B 6·71

C 465·17

D 470·12

15. Which of the following statements best describes a detritivore?

A Micro-organism with external enzymatic digestion

B Micro-organism with internal enzymatic digestion

C Invertebrate with external enzymatic digestion

D Invertebrate with internal enzymatic digestion

16. The release of nutrients from the remains of dead organisms in the soil is called

A assimilation

B humus formation

C mineralisation

D nitrification.

17. Which of the following promotes the loss of nitrogen from soil due to the activity of denitrifying bacteria?

A Leaching of nitrate from soil in drainage water

B Anaerobic conditions caused by water saturation

C High levels of phosphate from addition of fertilisers

D The presence of a leguminous crop such as clover

18. A flask containing a solution of ammonium salts was set up to demonstrate the activity of some of the micro-organisms involved in the nitrogen cycle. A sample of fresh soil was added to the solution and the concentration of nitrite measured over several weeks. The results are shown in the graph below.

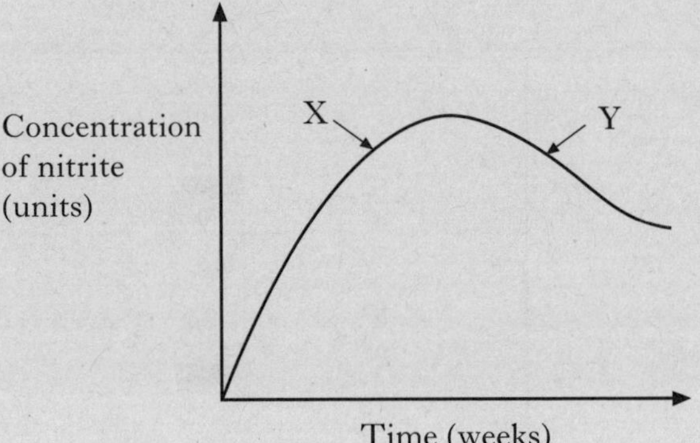

Which line in the table below correctly represents bacterial activity which can account for the changes shown at X and Y?

	Bacteria active at X	*Bacteria active at Y*
A	*Nitrosomonas*	*Rhizobium*
B	*Nitrobacter*	*Nitrosomonas*
C	*Nitrobacter*	*Rhizobium*
D	*Nitrosomonas*	*Nitrobacter*

19. Coral snakes are highly venomous and have a pattern of dark red, yellow and black bands.

This is an example of

A aposematic colouration

B Batesian mimicry

C camouflage

D Mullerian mimicry.

20. A species of Latin American ant inhabits the thorns of a species of *Acacia*. The ant receives nectar and shelter from the plant. The plant receives protection from the ants.

This is an example of

A parasitism

B commensalism

C mutualism

D predation.

21. *Hydra* is a small freshwater animal that uses its tentacles to catch food. One variety (green hydra) has photosynthetic algae living in its tissues. Another variety (colourless hydra) has no algae.

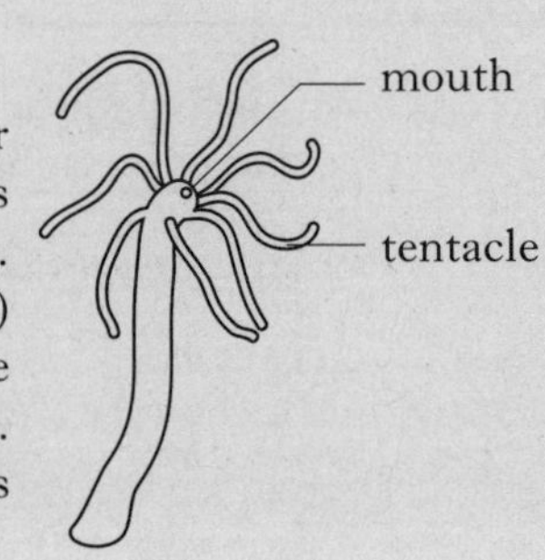

The relationship between *Hydra* and the algae is believed to be an example of mutualism.

Under what conditions would a comparison of the growth rates of green and colourless *Hydra* test this hypothesis?

A Light; food supplied

B Light; no food supplied

C Dark; food supplied

D Dark; no food supplied.

[Turn over

22. Animals may interact with their environment by conformation or regulation. Each statement below applies to one of these interactions.

1 A wide range of habitats can be occupied.
2 A restricted range of habitats can be occupied.
3 There is a high energy cost.
4 There is no energy cost.

Which statements apply to regulation?

A 1 and 3 only

B 1 and 4 only

C 2 and 3 only

D 2 and 4 only

23. The graph below shows primary productivity in a loch at different depths. Data were collected before and after an experiment in which phosphate was added to the loch.

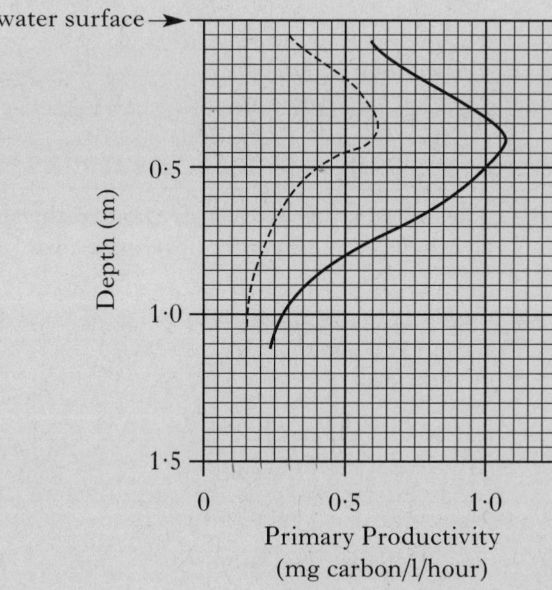

Calculate the percentage increase in productivity at a depth of 0·5 m that results from the addition of phosphate.

A 60%

B 75%

C 150%

D 300%

0·4 1·0

24. Which line in the table correctly identifies the effect of each pollutant?

	Biomagnification	*Eutrophication*	*Global warming*
A	phosphate	DDT	CFCs
B	DDT	phosphate	CFCs
C	CFCs	phosphate	DDT
D	DDT	CFCs	phosphate

25. The concentrations of some toxic organic chemicals in sea water were compared to concentrations known to produce lethal effects in laboratory experiments.

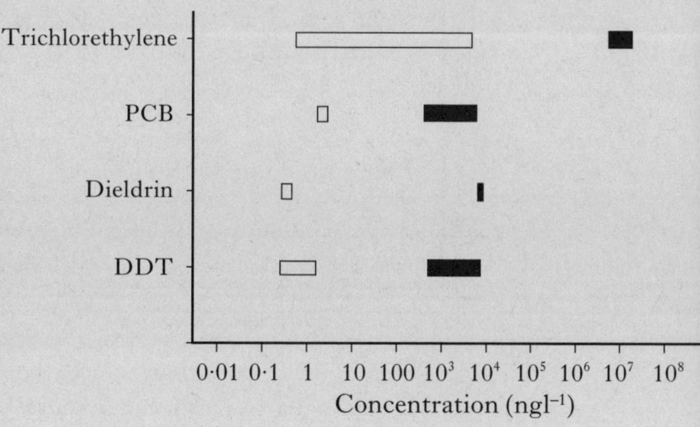

Which of the following is a valid conclusion from the data shown?

A All the toxic organic chemicals are found at lethal concentrations in sea water.

B Trichlorethylene is the only chemical found at lethal concentrations in sea water.

C DDT produces toxic effects in sea water due to biomagnification through the ecosystem.

D There is no evidence that the concentrations of toxic organic chemicals in sea water could produce lethal effects.

[*END OF SECTION A*]

Candidates are reminded that the answer sheet MUST be returned INSIDE the front cover of the answer book.

[Turn over for Section B on *Page ten*]

SECTION B

All questions in this section should be attempted.
All answers must be written clearly and legibly in ink.

1. The effects of large carnivores on ecosystems are not well understood. Predators can have a "top-down" effect that ripples down through the trophic levels below them. The effect is called a *trophic cascade*. In a trophic cascade a predatory species significantly affects consumer populations, which in turn results in significant changes at the producer level. Two recent studies in the USA have investigated trophic cascades.

One study investigated the effects of reintroducing wolves (*Canis lupus*) to Yellowstone National Park in 1994. The strength of the trophic cascade was assessed by measuring feeding damage caused by elk (*Cervus elaphus*) to saplings produced by regenerating aspen trees (*Populus tremuloides*) (Table 1).

In the second study, a trophic cascade was quantified in a comparison of two neighbouring canyons in Zion National Park. These two canyons, Zion Canyon and North Creek, have similar geology, climate and plant species but are visited by substantially different numbers of tourists. The Figure shows the age structure of populations of cottonwood trees (*Populus fremontii*) in the two canyons. The age of cottonwood trees was estimated by measuring their diameter at chest height. Other than the trees, the most significant species within the community are the predatory cougar (*Puma concolor)* and the herbivorous mule deer (*Odocoileus hemionus*).

To compare the abundance of these species in the two canyons, data were collected from two-metre-wide transects following the course of river and stream banks. Evidence of cougars, which are highly sensitive to human disturbance, was determined by searching for scats (droppings) along 4000m of walking trails in the two localities (Table 2).

Table 1 : Survey data for Yellowstone National Park

Year	*Wolf population*	*Elk population*	*Feeding damage* (%)	*Average aspen sapling height* (cm)
1993	0	17 500	No data	No data
1997	24	13 000	95	30
2001	74	12 000	80	50
2005	82	9000	20	170

Question 1 (continued)

Figure: Age structure of cottonwood trees in two canyons in Zion National Park

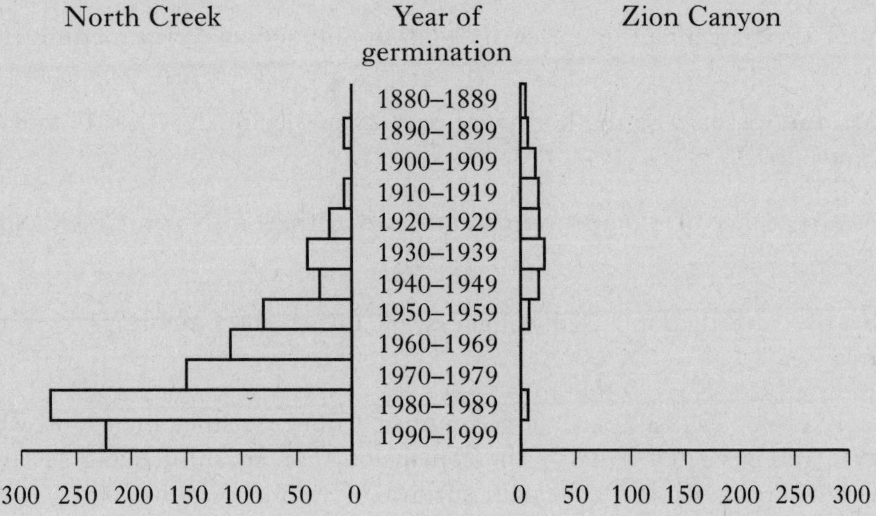

Table 2: Comparative data for three species in Zion National Park

	Canyon	
Species	*North Creek*	*Zion Canyon*
Cougar (scats per km)	1·75	0
Deer (hoof prints per km)	3·3	700
Young cottonwood (saplings per km)	900	23

[Question 1 continues on *Page twelve*

Marks

Question 1 (continued)

(*a*) Top-down effects are caused by heterotrophs. What is meant by the term heterotroph? **1**

(*b*) Using data from Table 1:

(i) describe the trophic cascade caused by the reintroduction of wolves; **2**

(ii) calculate the percentage increase in wolf population over the period 1997 to 2001; **1**

(iii) suggest **one** reason why the herbivore population declined by less than 8% over the same period. **1**

(*c*) Compare the abundance of old and young cottonwood trees in North Creek and Zion Canyon. **2**

(*d*) Suggest why the investigators used cougar scats rather than sightings to estimate cougar abundance. **1**

(*e*) Zion Canyon has been accessible to a large number of tourists since the 1930s, whereas North Creek is rarely visited. Justify the conclusion that, by influencing the trophic cascade, tourism is responsible for the poor survival of young cottonwoods. **2**

(*f*) (i) What term describes biotic effects that increase in intensity as the population in an area increases? **1**

(ii) Explain how the intensity of grazing can influence the *diversity* of plant species. **2**

(13)

[Questions 2, 3 and 4 are on fold-out *Page thirteen*

Marks

2. (*a*) Himalayan balsam (*Impatiens glandulifera*) is an exotic species that spread into Scotland after being introduced into the UK in 1839. Left unchecked it can form an ecologically harmful monoculture. Himalayan balsam is an annual plant (its whole life cycle takes place within one year). Seeds of this species can remain dormant in the soil for up to two years.

(i) What is the benefit of a period of dormancy in seeds? 1

(ii) Describe a damaging effect arising from the spread of an exotic species. 1

(iii) Suggest a method for controlling Himalayan balsam. 1

(iv) How would the seed dormancy of the Himalayan balsam affect the design of an eradication programme? 1

(*b*) Give **one** effect on soil when monoculture is used in intensive food production. 1

(5)

3. Explain how the use of fossil fuels disrupts the symbiotic relationship in coral. **(4)**

4. (*a*) Why is competition regarded as a negative interaction? 1

(*b*) Explain what is meant by a fundamental niche. 1

(*c*) A survey of birds in the Bismarck Islands, Papua New Guinea, found that two similar species of cuckoo-doves, *Macropygia mackinlayi* and *M. nigrirostris*, are never found breeding on the same island.

M. mackinlayi

M. nigrirostris

The two species are believed to have very similar fundamental niches. Suggest an explanation for the two species occupying different islands. 2

(*d*) Parasites may be transmitted between closely related species.

(i) Why is the transmission of parasites less common between **unrelated** species? 1

(ii) State **one** way in which parasites can be transmitted. 1

(6)

Marks

5. The diagram below shows a section of plasma membrane with proteins labelled A to E.

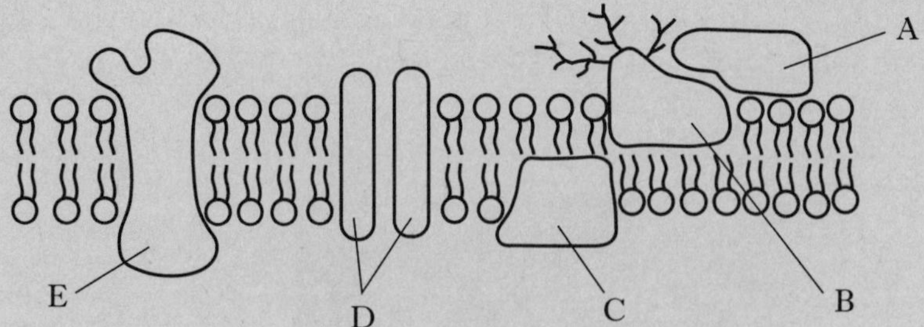

(*a*) (i) Identify which of the proteins A to E are integral membrane proteins. **1**

(ii) Which type of signalling molecule requires a receptor protein at the cell surface? **1**

(*b*) The membranes of most eukaryotic cells contain a proportion of the steroid cholesterol.

(i) Describe the general structure of a steroid. **1**

(ii) State **one** role of cholesterol in membranes. **1**

(iii) The table below shows the proportion of cholesterol in membranes from different locations.

Membrane location	*Proportion of cholesterol* (g cholesterol per g membrane)
Liver plasma membrane	0·18
Mitochondrial membrane	0·03
Endoplasmic reticulum	0·06

Show, as a simple whole number ratio, the relative amounts of cholesterol in liver plasma membrane, mitochondrial membrane and endoplasmic reticulum. **1**

(5)

Marks

6. Binding of specific proteins to DNA is important in the control of gene expression.

(*a*) Describe the effect of repressor protein binding to DNA in the *lac* operon. **1**

(*b*) Binding to DNA of the *engrailed* protein of the fruit fly *Drosophila melanogaster* is required during development of the fruit fly embryo.

The DNA-binding region of the engrailed protein consists of a stretch of sixty amino acids that contain two α-helices connected by a short extended chain of amino acids as shown in Figure 1.

Figure 1

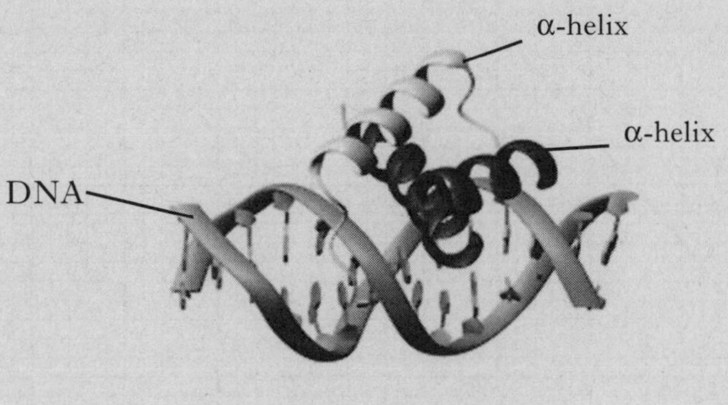

α-helix

α-helix

DNA

(i) What level of protein structure is an α-helix? **1**

(ii) The side chains of the amino acids within the α-helix regions interact directly with DNA. Figure 2 shows the amino acids in a short stretch of one of the α-helix regions of the engrailed protein.

Figure 2

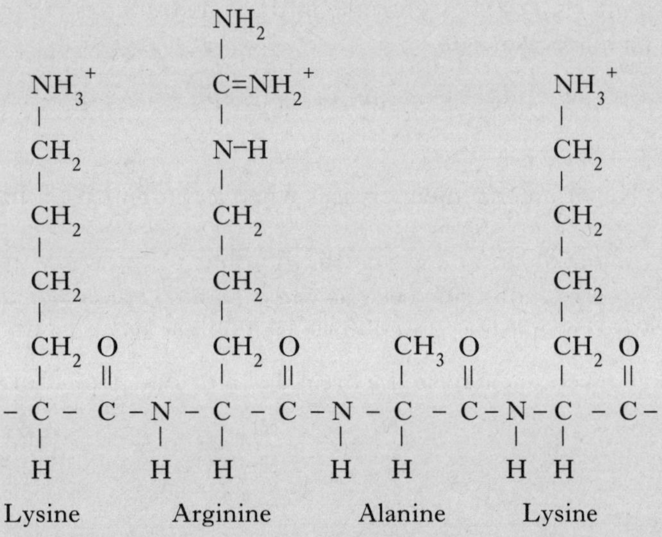

```
                    NH2
                    |
  NH3+              C=NH2+                        NH3+
  |                 |                             |
  CH2               N-H                           CH2
  |                 |                             |
  CH2               CH2                           CH2
  |                 |                             |
  CH2               CH2                           CH2
  |                 |                             |
  CH2  O            CH2  O         CH3  O         CH2  O
  |    ||           |    ||        |    ||        |    ||
– C –  C – N –  C – C – N –  C –  C – N – C  –  C –
  |        |    |        |   |        |   |
  H        H    H        H   H        H   H
Lysine       Arginine        Alanine      Lysine
```

Name the class of amino acid to which lysine belongs. **1**

(iii) The binding region of the engrailed protein contains a high proportion of lysine residues. Suggest how the presence of these amino acids would assist in the binding of the engrailed protein to DNA. **1**

(4)

[Turn over

Marks

7. Enzyme kinetics is the study of the rate of enzyme-catalysed reactions.
The graph below shows the rates of the reaction for the enzyme penicillinase over a range of substrate concentrations. The substrate is penicillin.

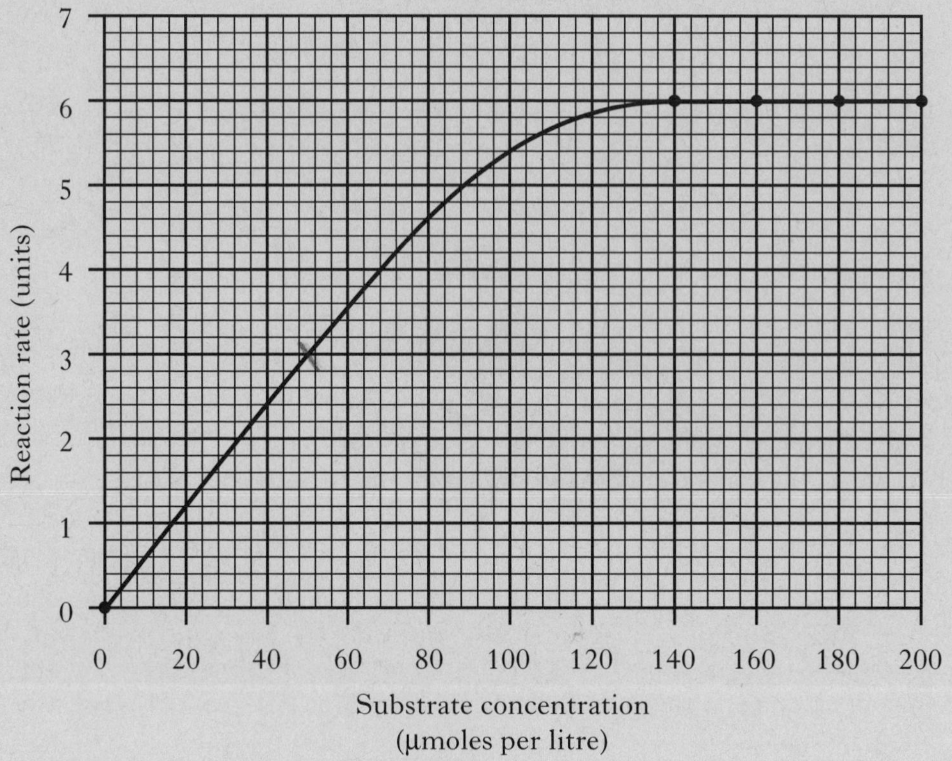

The Michaelis constant (K_m) of an enzyme is the substrate concentration at which the reaction rate is half its maximum rate.

(*a*) Calculate the K_m of penicillinase assuming the graph shows that the maximum rate has been reached. **1**

(*b*) Explain why the K_m of an enzyme increases when a competitive inhibitor is present. **1**

(*c*) The turnover number of an enzyme is the number of substrate molecules converted into product by an enzyme in one second when an enzyme is working at its maximum rate. The turnover number for penicillinase is 2000 per second.

Calculate the time taken to catalyse the breakdown of one penicillin molecule. **1**

(3)

8. Answer **either** A **or** B.

A. Describe the structure of the monosaccharide glucose. Discuss the structures and functions of the main polysaccharides made using glucose as a monomer. **(15)**

OR

B. Give an account of the processes involved in the polymerase chain reaction (PCR) and DNA profiling. **(15)**

[*END OF SECTION B*]

SECTION C

Candidates should attempt questions on one unit, either Biotechnology or Animal Behaviour or Physiology, Health and Exercise.

The questions on Animal Behaviour can be found on pages 20–23.

The questions on Physiology, Health and Exercise can be found on pages 24–26.

All answers must be written clearly and legibly in ink.

Labelled diagrams may be used where appropriate.

BIOTECHNOLOGY *Marks*

1. The Figure below shows the final stage in a test that confirms a blood sample contains antibodies against *Herpes simplex* virus (HSV). HSV antigen is attached to the plastic well and any unbound areas are coated with non-reactive material.

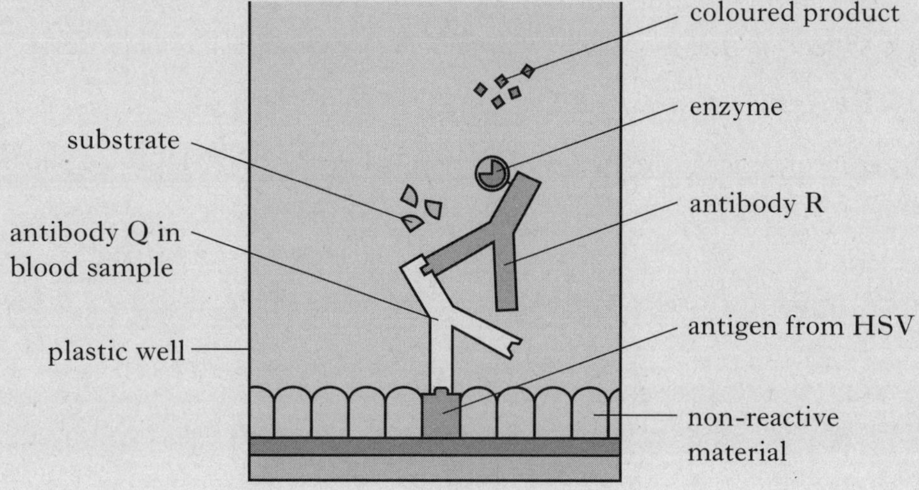

(*a*) (i) Identify the technique represented in the diagram. **1**

(ii) Explain why the test represented would not reveal if the person had been infected with chickenpox virus. **1**

(iii) Use information in the Figure to explain why inadequate rinsing just before the stage shown might result in a *false* positive result. **2**

(*b*) Antibody R was produced commercially in a fermenter from hybridoma cells.

What **two** cell types are combined to make hybridoma cells? **1**

(5)

[Turn over

BIOTECHNOLOGY **(continued)** *Marks*

2. The flow chart shows steps involved in the manufacture of yoghurt.

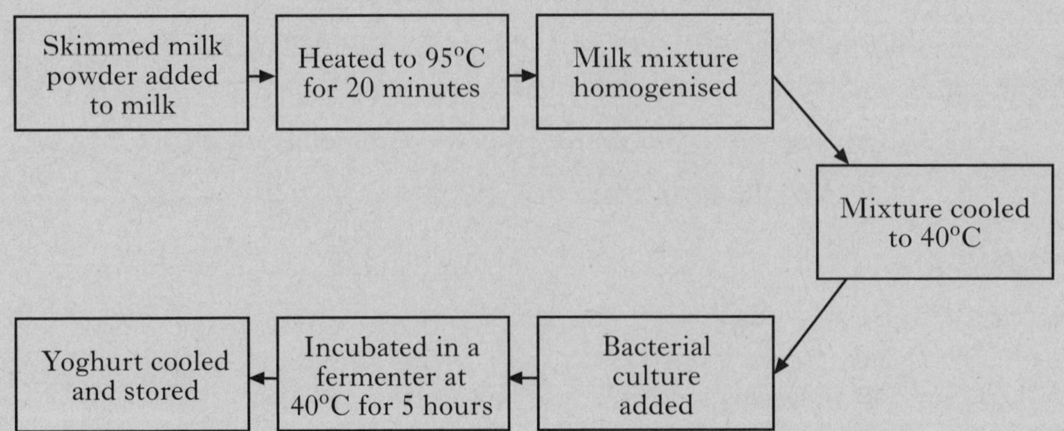

(*a*) The milk mixture is heated to 95 °C for 20 minutes to remove dissolved oxygen.

(i) What chemical conversion is promoted by the anaerobic conditions? **1**

(ii) Give a further reason for the heat treatment at this stage. **1**

(*b*) During incubation in the fermenter, yoghurt samples were removed and examined under a microscope. The figure below shows the field of view.

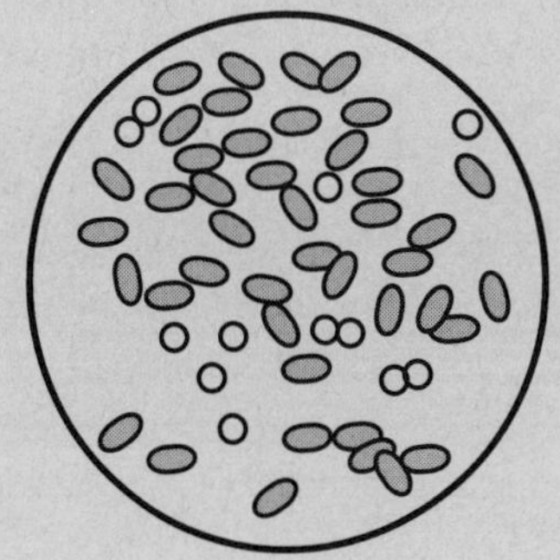

(i) What can be observed? **1**

(ii) Account for the observation. **1**

(4)

3. Describe the scaling up process required to produce a suitable volume of pure bacterial culture for an industrial fermenter. **(5)**

***BIOTECHNOLOGY* (continued)** *Marks*

4. Silage is used for winter feeding of farm animals and is commonly made by wrapping baled grass in polythene. Ensilage of plants in this way preserves the nutritional quality by limiting protein breakdown.

(*a*) Apart from wrapping bales, give **one** other method of making silage. 1

(*b*) Explain how changes that take place within the wrapped bale help to preserve the silage. 2

(*c*) Name a bacterial species that would be added before the baled grass is wrapped. 1

(*d*) In a study involving ensilage of harvested lupin plants, researchers evaluated the effect of adding bacteria to the bales. The graphs below show the data obtained. Error bars show variation between replicates.

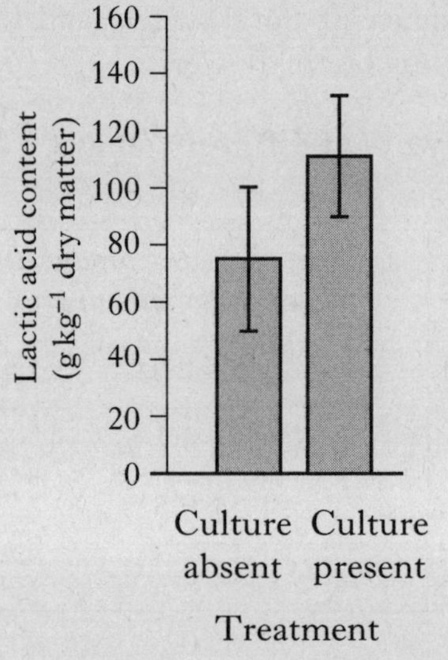

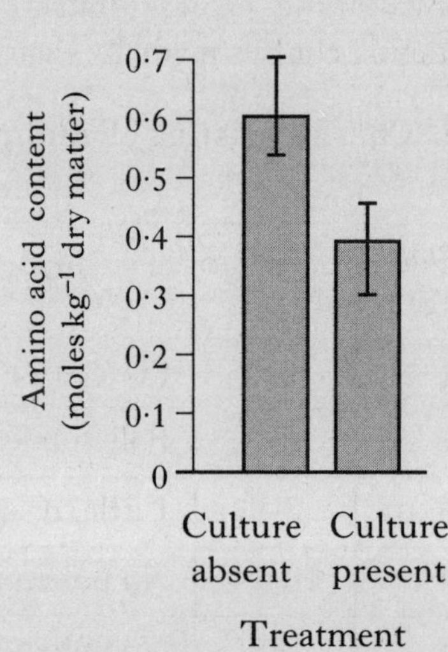

(i) What evidence supports the conclusion that the treatment with bacteria preserves the nutritional quality of the plant material? 1

(ii) Draw **one** other conclusion about the effect of adding bacteria to fermenting silage. 1

(6)

(20)

[End of *Biotechnology* questions. *Animal Behaviour* questions start on Page 20]

SECTION C (continued)

Marks

ANIMAL BEHAVIOUR

1. The eastern spinebill (*Acanthorhyncus tenuirostris*) is a small bird from eastern Australia. One of its major foods is nectar from the mountain correa (*Correa lawrenciana*).

Figure 1: Eastern spinebill feeding on mountain correa

(*a*) In a study of eastern spinebill foraging, flowers of mountain correa were assigned to different developmental stages (Floral stages 1–5). Some characteristics of each stage are shown in the Table. Figure 2 shows the abundance of floral stages available and the foraging choices made by eastern spinebills feeding on the flowers.

Table: Characteristics of mountain correa flowers at different stages

Floral stage	*Age* (days)	*Pollen production*	*Volume of nectar produced per flower over 24 hours* (μ l)
1	1–2	Pollen present, not released	1·0
2	3–7	Pollen released	3·1
3	8–9	Little, if any, pollen present	0·5
4	10–13	No pollen	0
5	14+	No pollen	0

ANIMAL BEHAVIOUR **(continued)** *Marks*

1. (*a*) **(continued)**

Figure 2: Proportions of floral stages available and foraging choices made by eastern spinebills

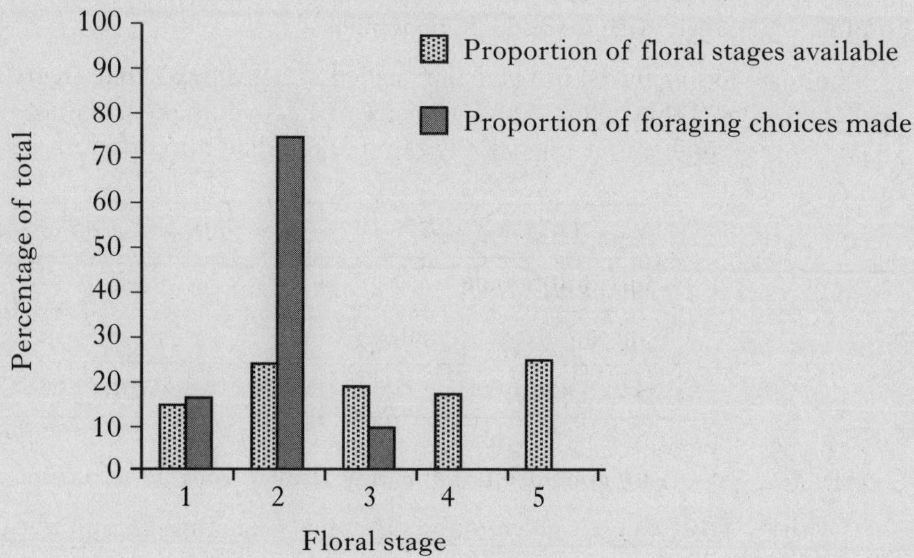

(i) Use the data in Figure 2 to compare floral stages 2 and 5. **2**

(ii) What is meant by the term optimal foraging? **1**

(iii) How does the information provided in both the Table and Figure 2 demonstrate optimal foraging in spinebills? **1**

(*b*) The eastern spinebill's nest is a small cup made mainly from twigs, grass, bark, feathers and spider webs. Only the female builds the nest and incubates the eggs but both parents feed the young after they have hatched.

(i) This information suggests greater investment by the female parent. Describe another way in which female investment is likely to be greater than that of the male parent. **1**

(ii) Explain how nest building in the eastern spinebill provides an example of an extended phenotype. **1**

(*c*) The eastern spinebill does not show any marked sexual dimorphism.

Figure 1 shows a male bird. What would the female bird look like in comparison? **1**

(7)

[Turn over

ANIMAL BEHAVIOUR **(continued)** *Marks*

2. The silk produced by female spiders often contains chemical deposits that provide males with important information about species identity, age, sex and the reproductive status of a female.

Female wolf spiders *Schizocosa ocreata* rarely mate with more than one male and, once they have mated, are more likely to cannibalise (eat) males. Males, on the other hand, will often try to mate with more than one female.

The male has a courtship behaviour called a "jerky tap" that elicits a reaction from the female. The Table below shows measurements of the time taken for males to produce the jerky tap response after exposure to samples of silks from different origins.

Origin of silk	*Time until jerky tap response* (s)
Subadult female	155
Unmated adult female	22
Mated adult female	105

(*a*) (i) State **one** conclusion that can be drawn from these results. 1

(ii) What name is given to the delay between stimulus and response? 1

(iii) Name another aspect of this jerky tap response that could be observed and used for comparison. 1

(iv) Suggest **one** disadvantage of laboratory-based research into animal behaviour. 1

(*b*) The "selfish gene" concept maintains that individual organisms should behave so as to maximise the survival of copies of their genes.

Give **one** reason why the genes responsible for a male spider's response to silk in the selection of a mate can be described as "selfish". 1

(5)

***ANIMAL BEHAVIOUR* (continued)** *Marks*

3. Cheetahs (*Acinonyx jubatus*) in the Serengeti National Park in Tanzania kill more male Thomson's gazelles (*Gazella thomsoni*) than would be expected from the sex ratio of the local gazelle population.

The Table below shows data obtained by observing groups of Thomson's gazelles.

	males	*females*
Proportion on periphery of group (%)	75	53
Nearest neighbour distance (m)	9·3	4·6
Proportion of time spent scanning with head up (%)	8·4	11·4
Proportion in population (%)	30	70
Proportion hunted (%)	63	37

(*a*) Suggest why male Thomson's gazelles are more likely than females to be selected as prey by hunting cheetahs. **1**

(*b*) Calculate the number of males on the periphery of a group of 80 gazelles. **1**

(*c*) What name is given to the scanning behaviour? **1**

(3)

4. Describe how appeasement and ritualised displays in agonistic interactions can benefit all members of social groups. Illustrate your answer by reference to named species. **(5)**

(20)

[End of *Animal Behaviour* questions. *Physiology, Health and Exercise* questions start on Page 24]

[Turn over

SECTION C (continued) *Marks*

PHYSIOLOGY, HEALTH AND EXERCISE

1. (*a*) The graph shows obesity data for England in 1993 and 2002.

Individuals were described as obese if they had a body mass index (BMI) of 30 or greater.

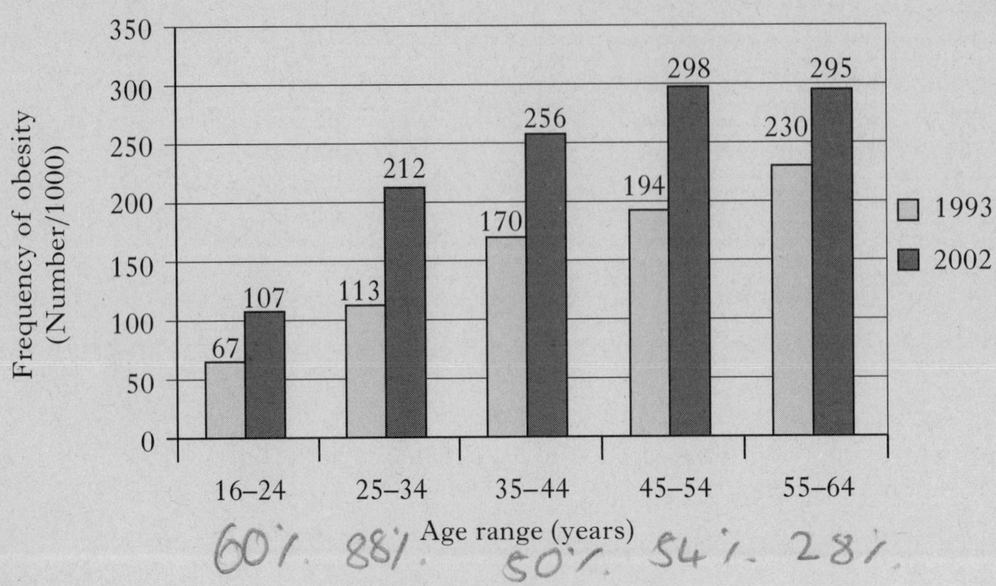

(i) What two measurements are needed to calculate BMI? **1**

(ii) Obesity has increased in all age ranges over the ten year period.

Which age range has shown the biggest percentage increase? **1**

(iii) Give **one** other general trend shown by the data. **1**

(iv) Name **one** medical condition for which obesity is a risk factor. **1**

(*b*) (i) Bioelectrical impedance analysis (BIA) is a method used to determine percentage body fat. Outline the principle on which this method is based. **2**

(ii) Give **one** limitation of BIA. **1**

(7)

2. Discuss the changes that take place in the cardiovascular system during a short period of strenuous exercise. **(4)**

PHYSIOLOGY, HEALTH AND EXERCISE **(continued)** *Marks*

3. The Bruce protocol is a method used in maximal exercise testing to determine fitness. A subject wearing an oxygen-monitoring mask is supervised running on a treadmill while the gradient (slope) and speed of the treadmill are both increased in a standard way. When the subject is exhausted, the time is noted.

The Table below shows some results from a study using this method. The values have been selected for four young healthy males who each took the same time to reach exhaustion.

Time (min)	*Body mass* (kg)	*Maximum oxygen uptake* ($l\,min^{-1}$)	*Fitness* ($ml\,kg^{-1}\,min^{-1}$)
10·5	70	2·53	36·2
10·5	75	2·72	36·2
10·5	85	3·08	36·2
10·5	90	3·26	36·2

(*a*) Explain why measuring oxygen uptake is a valid way to assess fitness. **2**

(*b*) Explain why the "Fitness" measurement is independent of body mass. **1**

(*c*) Calculate the maximum oxygen uptake of an 80 kg male who took 10·5 minutes to reach exhaustion in the same test. **1**

(*d*) Give an example of a situation where the individual given a treadmill test would **not** be stressed to exhaustion. **1**

(5)

[Turn over for Question 4 on *Page twenty-six*

***PHYSIOLOGY, HEALTH AND EXERCISE* (continued)** *Marks*

4. In an investigation into energy expenditure measured by direct calorimetry, subjects at rest were given a solution of either glucose or sucrose (a disaccharide). The results are shown in the graph below.

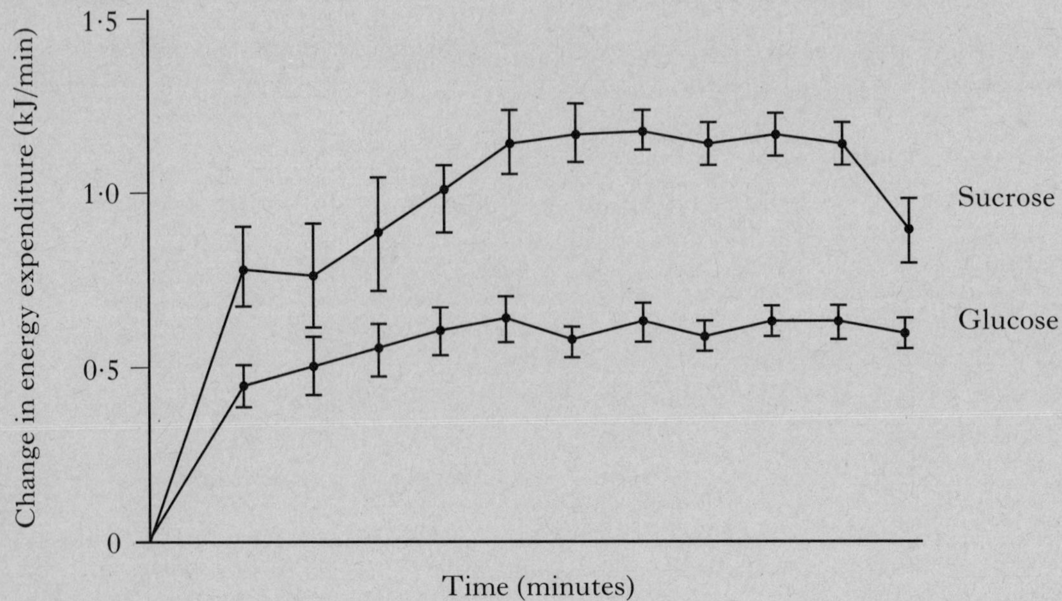

(*a*) Which component of total energy expenditure is being investigated in this study? **1**

(*b*) What evidence is there that diet affects energy expenditure? **1**

(*c*) What do the error bars in the graph indicate about the results presented? **1**

(*d*) The results in this investigation were obtained by direct calorimetry.

Give **one** way in which indirect calorimetry differs from direct calorimetry. **1**

(4)

(20)

[*END OF QUESTION PAPER*]

[BLANK PAGE]

Acknowledgements

Permission has been sought from all relevant copyright holders and Bright Red Publishing is grateful for the use of the following:

An extract from 'From structure to disease: the evolving tale of aquaporin biology' by Landon S. King, David Kozono and Peter Agre, taken from *Nature Reviews Molecular Cell Biology* 1 Sept 2004. Copyright © 2004, Nature Publishing Group (2008 page 10);

A table adapted from 'Diffusional water permeability of human erythrocytes and their ghosts' by J Brahm, 1982. Taken from *The Journal of General Physiology 79* © J Brahm/The Journal of General Physiology (2008 page 10);

A picture from *Physiological Mini-Reviews* Vol 1, No 10, May 2006 by A Guttierrez. Published by The Argentine Physiological Society (2008 page 10);

A picture from 'Severely Impaired Urinary Concentrating Ability in Transgenic Mice Lacking Aquaporin-1 Water Channels' by Tonghui Ma, Baoxue Yang, Annemarie Gillespie, Elaine J. Carlson, Charles J. Epstein and A. S. Verkman. Published in *Journal of Biological Chemistry* 20 February 1998. Copyright © 1998, by the American Society for Biochemistry and Molecular Biology (2008 page 11).